CAT NO. SON0584

Written by
Catherine Curzon

Ben Gazur

April Madden

Alice Pattillo

Proof reader: Cameron Thurlow

Images courtesy of
Getty Images

Alamy

© Creative Commons/Ethan Doyle White

© Creative Commons/Chris Gladis

© Creative Commons/ Таролог Альбина

© Creative Commons/Roberto Viesi

© Creative Commons/Covetrick

Made in EU.

ISBN: 978-1-915343-46-8

THE COMPLETE BEGINNER'S GUIDE TO TAROT

Cut the deck and draw your first card. The Page of Swords – you are curious and bold. And the second? The Hermit. A seeker after truth, prepared to venture forth to find it. The third and final card? The World. You shall find the answers you seek, and your curiosity will be fulfilled.

For centuries, tarot has offered its practitioners a resource to ask questions about their fate and that of the people and the world around them. For some it's a meditative exercise, for others a magical tool. In this book you'll discover its sometimes surprising history, and how it went from an ordinary card game to one of the world's most famous divination tools. You'll learn the occult secrets behind the imagery of the cards and discover who put them there, and why. Plus, you'll find an in-depth guide to the meanings of the 22 cards of the Major Arcana and the 56 cards in the suits of the Minor Arcana, and easy-to-follow diagrams and guides to the most popular kinds of card readings, so that you too can interpret the mysteries of the tarot.

sona BOOKS

CONTENTS

THE
HISTORY

The story behind the fateful cards
and their use today

THE
HISTORY
OF
TAROT

Tarot cards have been around for centuries, in a variety of guises. From ancient Egypt to today, they continue to evolve

Tarot has lived many lives over many centuries, and it has evolved through different cultures, beliefs and practices just as it continues to do today. Every person who has ever picked up a deck has done so for their own personal reasons, and the cards in their hands have served as anything from a game to tools of sacred divination and connection, to instruments of self-discovery and reflection. Today, tarot has evolved far beyond its gaming origins, until many people wouldn't even know that the cards ever even had that purpose. Instead, tarot cards are now more often recognised as the purview of fortune tellers, occultists, and those who seek to divine the future.

Tarot's process of morphing from a favourite of Italian card players to an essential tool of psychic practitioners and even counsellors and life coaches, was not completed overnight. Nor was it the result of one major shift, but rather a gradual process over the centuries that saw the cards change not only in appearance, but use too.

The timeline of tarot history isn't only the evolution of an art form and a card game into something more though. In fact, it is also a timeline of changing focus and sensibilities in three centuries of cultural shifts. From changes made to card imagery to satisfy religious sensitivities to the emergence of new tarot decks, spiritual movements and occult groups who sought to use the cards to serve their own beliefs, the growth of tarot illuminates the changing relationship of our own interaction with the cards that had once been the playing pieces in a game.

From its early days, when only the pips were in use, to the addition of the allegorical trump cards all the way to today's endless selection of deck, the cards continue to fascinate as much in the 21st century as they did in the days of the Renaissance.

A TAROT TIMELINE

A DIARY ENTRY
1440

A diarist in Florence, Italy, makes the first recognised reference to tarot cards in his diary. Though brief, it provides concrete evidence that the cards were in use in the 15th century.

THE VISCONTI-SFORZA
1451

The Visconti-Sforza tarot is a collection of more than a dozen incomplete tarot decks from Renaissance Italy. This collection is believed to contain the oldest tarot decks still in existence.

FRANCE ADOPTS THE TAROT
1499

In 1499, French soldiers conquer and occupy Italian lands and there they encounter the tarot cards, a popular form of entertainment in Italy. By now mass printed and readily available to buy, the French snap up their own decks and take them and the game of tarot home to France. Card manufacturers soon adopt the suits to reflect those of their own playing cards, namely hearts, diamonds, clubs and spades, all of which are considered easier for card manufacturers to reproduce as they begin to produce their own tarot decks for sale.

TAROCCHI
EARLY 1500s

Whether it is tarocchi or tarrochini, enthusiasm for the card games that utilise the tarot decks flourishes across Europe. As its popularity grows, so too does the number of decks available.

From trionfi to tarot

The decks of tarot cards that we know today weren't always used for divination. In fact, they came out of the world of gaming

Today, the tarot is immediately recognisable by its allegorical imagery and four suits, regardless of which of the innumerable decks available a reader chooses. Though widely used for divination across the world however, tarot cards have their foundations not in mysticism, but in card games.

Some scholars have argued about the exact origin of tarot, and just how far back one can trace it, with some arguing that its history can be traced through the mists of time back to ancient Egypt or beyond. Though these stories are certainly tantalising and hint at the deeper mysticism that many have sought in the deceptively simple deck of cards, there is little evidence to support these claims. In fact, what truths exist regarding the earliest existence of tarot did not emerge until the 15th century, when tarot cards were first referred to as playing cards and used in the courts of Europe's wealthiest nobles. In a time before mass-printing was available to the majority, to own a deck of tarot cards was a symbol of wealth and prestige. After all, it took money to be able to commission artists to create the richly illustrated tarot cards that the nobles used for their games.

They built on the foundations of traditional playing cards, the origins of which are murky. The first references to a deck of playing cards can be found in Berne in 1367, but nothing is known about these early cards beyond the fact that they existed. However, a 14th century text reveals that a deck of cards consisted of four suits, each containing 13 cards. In Italy, these suits were clubs, coins, cups and swords, though suits would differ depending on the geographical region. Just like modern decks of playing cards, they lacked the illustrated trump cards exclusive to tarot, that eventually became known as the Major Arcana.

Exactly how cards evolved from playing cards to tarot is lost to the mists of time. However, scholars agree that the first tarot decks appear to have emerged from Milan in the middle of the 15th century. These Italian decks adapted the traditional Italian playing card suits of clubs, coins, cups and swords. In each suit, there were conventional pips, or numbered cards, and face, the king, queen, knight and knave. There was also the Fool, a wild card and, alongside these traditional elements of playing cards were a series of 21 allegorically illustrated cards, known as the trionfi or triumph, which was later further shortened to trumps. The first known reference to the trionfi cards can be found in the written records of the Florentine court, where two decks were under discussion in 1440.

However, though trump cards are certainly a fundamental part of the Italian games of tarocchi, trump cards did not appear to have originated in Italy. In fact, the earliest known example of a trump game comes with the German game of karnöffel, which was played as early as 1420. That game bears no other relation to those played with the tarot cards though. Once the Italian decks were assembled with their pips, faces and trumps, these so-called carta da trionfi were used to play the game of tarocchi and its derivative, tarocchini, which is still played today in Naples. Tarot games have been played since at least 1440, when the first surviving written reference to tarocchi was made.

> Tarot cards have their foundations not in mysticism but in card games

Today, tarot games remain a popular pastime in modern France. Curiously, they never caught on across the English Channel

"Tarot games are examples of trick taking games and the rules are complex"

Whereas earlier decks of playing cards were comprised of the four suits mentioned above, or localised variations of the suits, the addition of the trump cards allowed for a wider variation of games to be played. Indeed, the trump cards are vital for a game of tarocchi and its associated spin-offs, all of which utilise the trumps theme in their rules.

Tarot games are examples of trick taking games, and the rules are complex and difficult to master. This complexity did nothing to slow the flourishing popularity of the cards though and when French soldiers arrived in Italy in the closing days of the 15th century, they were as keen as anybody to sample the favourite games of locals. It was they who brought tarot cards home to France after the occupation of Milan, aiding in tarot's proliferation throughout the continent. As word of the new game spread through France and beyond, tarot began to thrive across Europe. It spread from territory to territory with travellers and as it did, its name and appearance evolved in subtle ways, according to local dialects and sensibilities.

The spread of tarot also depended in large part on industrial growth. Those early packs that were commissioned by Italian nobles were hand drawn and painted and exclusively available to the rich. Woodblock printing enabled more people to obtain their own set of tarot cards, as did the development of the printing press. These technologies placed tarot cards within reach of the person in the street, aiding in the game's growing popularity.

As the decks began to change to reflect the territories where they were used and their names subtly altered with each geographical region, tarot games soon became familiar in virtually every corner of Europe. In Germany the cards were known as tarock cards, whilst in France they were called tarot decks, the name by which they are known today across the world. Tarot games remain popular today in some parts of Europe, particularly Italy and France. Curiously though, the card games never really caught on in the United Kingdom.

ICONOGRAPHY AND SUITS

Just as the name of the tarot decks changed according to the countries where they were being used, so too did the iconography and suit symbols change too, to reflect local taste and tradition.

Each deck is made up of four suits, each containing numbered pips and court cards, and the trumps, which became the Minor and Major Arcana respectively. Whilst the pips remained constant due to their numerical nature, the suits of cards themselves varied according to location. Whilst the French initially favoured traditional clubs, spades, hearts and diamonds, Italian traditional card suits were those that eventually became the four suits of the Minor Arcana: namely coins (the pentacles of tarot), cups, swords and clubs (wands).

Likewise, the trump cards were subject to change in different countries too, to reflect local tradition or even religious sensitivities. Some Catholic countries chose to replace the Pope with a different card altogether, preferring not to use the Holy Father in their card games. Likewise, the Papesse of some decks was removed to protect the delicate sensibilities of those who preferred not to contemplate a female Pope, and replaced with characters including the Spanish Captain, a popular figure from the *Commedia dell'Arte*.

Local and religious sensitivities led to some tarot decks being amended. The Papesse was removed in order to avoid clashes with the Catholic church

II

LA·PAPESSE

A TAROT TIMELINE

THE NOBLET DECK
1660

More than a century after tarot came to France, Parisian Jean Noblet publishes the forerunner of the famous Tarot of Marseilles. It becomes a popular and influential deck amongst French tarot enthusiasts.

THE VATICAN INTERVENES
1725

As concern grows regarding some of the imagery in the tarot in Catholic regions, the Vatican demands that the Pope, the Papesse, the Empress and the Emperor are replaced with different cards in Bologna.

THE TAROT OF MARSEILLES
1736

François Chosson, a master engraver from Marseilles, designs the influential Tarot of Marseilles. It becomes the foundation stone of standard tarot decks and is adopted by occultists, who seek to expand the use of tarot beyond mere gaming.

DIVINATION
1789

French occultist Etteilla begins using the tarot cards for divination as an extension of his ongoing interest in cartomancy. He is the first recognised professional tarot reader and in 1789 creates his own "Hermetic" tarot cards, later adopted by other occult groups. Etteilla's interpretations are eventually published over a decade later, enabling others to learn how to read the tarot according to his methods. As novice card readers attempt to master the art of tarot reading, Etteilla's readings become the basis for the interpretations of the Minor Arcana, and are still in evidence in card meanings and readings today.

Reading the cards

For centuries thought of as just a card game, the tarot cards seemed to some to offer a doorway to the divine

Cartomancy, or the art of using playing cards to practice divination, has been a popular pastime for those who like to dabble in the mystical for several centuries. Yet cartomancers didn't initially use a special deck, but instead needed nothing more than a standard deck of playing cards. In fact, it wouldn't be until the 18th century that the tarot cards themselves entered the purview of mystics and occultists.

In 1781, a French clergyman named Antoine Court, who went by the far more mysterious-sounding name of Court de Gébelin, first attempted to interpret the cards of the tarot deck as something more mystical. He identified what he claimed were ancient Egyptian motifs on the cards and explained that these hinted at meanings far beyond those which had so far been imagined. Court de Gébelin believed that primitive humanity had once existed as an enlightened society with knowledge of mysticism and the divine that far outstripped those of his era. He laid out his theories in a 1781 volume of his immense collection of writings on his pet theories, *Le Monde Primitif*.

The very first time he had seen a tarot deck, de Gébelin wrote, he knew instinctively that its influence was not European, but ancient Egyptian. Though he had no evidence to back up his theory and was going entirely from his own gut feeling, de Gébelin believed beyond a doubt that the iconography on the cards had been encoded by ancient Egyptian priests, who had hidden within them the secrets of the *Book of Thoth*, the writings of the Egyptian god of wisdom. That knowledge, concealed within the imagery of tarot, had been brought to the Vatican, from whence it was eventually brought to France in the 14th century. In Court de Gébelin's theory, the cards enjoyed in games across the continent were actually repositories of magic. Court de Gébelin's book included an essay from the Comte de Mellet, in which the first connections are drawn between the tarot trump cards, the Kabbalah and the Hebrew alphabet, and suggesting that cartomancers should turn their studies to this as-yet unexplored avenue for occult divination. According to Court de Gébelin's book, this was how the ancient Egyptians themselves utilised the tarot.

The cartomancer who truly heeded that suggestion was Jean-Baptiste Alliette, a mystic who went by the name Etteilla, his surname in reverse. Etteilla had been practising cartomancy using a shortened deck of regular playing cards supplemented by his own Etteilla card. The release of Court de Gébelin's book riled Etteilla, who believed that de Gébelin was trespassing on his territory and, in 1785, he released his own book as a reply. In *How to Entertain Yourself with Tarot Cards*, Etteilla claimed that he had been working with the cards for thirty years before de Gébelin put pen to paper.

Court de Gébelin and Etteilla alike used the Tarot of

> According to de Gébelin the tarot cards were actually repositories of magic

Etteilla popularised the use of tarot to divine the future. He wrote books, produced cards and even started up a magical school

Marseilles deck for their initial work, but Etteilla soon found that it wasn't quite suited to his personal needs. After the release of his book, Etteilla made the study of his tarot the centre of his work. He formed a group to discuss the cards and their meanings and, in 1789, published his own customised deck. This new deck combined Hermetic mysticism with Etteilla's personal interests in French methods of cartomancy and was the very first deck to be designed specifically for occult use. The book and deck excited so much interest amongst French students of the occult that Etteilla founded his own

Court de Gébelin believed that the tarot cards contained the hidden mysticism of ancient Egypt, and the teachings of the god Thoth himself

New School of Magic, at which he taught students the secrets of the *Book of Thoth*, essentially how to unlock the hidden secrets of the tarot cards.

Etteilla's influence on modern tarot cannot be understated. In 1790 he published *Theoretical and Practical Course in the Book of Thoth*, in which he laid out his interpretations of what eventually became the Major and Minor Arcana, sprinkling his theories with liberal amounts of astrology and linking the cards and their suits to the zodiac and the four elements. Tarot readings became more and more fashionable thanks to celebrity cartomancers such as Marie Anne Adelaide Lenormand, who read the cards for royalty and celebrities and became so popular that after her death, a posthumous tie-in deck was released that bore her name.

The history of tarot as a divination tool was written in the 18th and 19th century as occultist after occultist built on the work of their forerunners and contemporaries. Just as Court de Gébelin's entirely evidence-free Egyptian explanation was followed by Etteilla's writings, demonstrations and school, each practitioner brought something of themselves and their beliefs to tarot divination.

The final piece of the puzzle was placed by the French author Jean-Baptiste Pitois, who wrote under the name Paul Christian.

When Christian began to use the tarot, the deck was simply divided into the trumps and the pips. It was Christian who coined the terms Major and Minor Arcana in 1870, lending an extra air of mysticism. In his book, *The History and Practice of Magic*, he further combined Egyptian mysticism with elements of other faiths and Hermetic practice to deepen the mysteries of the tarot. Unfortunately, Christian had a habit of misquoting or simply making up sources and attributing them to ancient texts. Despite their dubious origins, however, his writings proved highly influential.

After centuries as nothing more than a game, by the time the 20th century dawned, tarot was indelibly linked with divination. It was a fashion and practice that would only continue as the new century began.

ÉLIPHAS LÉVI

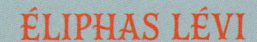

Born Alphonse Louis Constant, Éliphas Lévi was a French occultist and author who specialised in esoteric interests. His teachings had a fundamental impact on the Hermetic Order of the Golden Dawn and he created the fearsome goat-headed image of Baphomet.

Lévi developed his own system of ceremonial magic, which he believed would bridge the gap between faith and science. Incorporating alchemy, astrology and the Kabbalah, his own version of magic was not particularly new, but he added an element that others hadn't: the tarot. He constructed a narrative which linked the Major Arcana to the 22 letters of the Hebrew alphabet and the Tree of Life, and suggested that the four suits represented the four Hebrew letters that spelled God's name. He was the first to employ tarot not only as a standalone card system, but as a fundamental element of a much larger whole, which encompassed heaven, earth and everything in between.

Éliphas Lévi set down his beliefs in his 1856 book, Dogma and the Ritual of Transcendental Magic. When the book crossed the sea to England, Lévi's interpretations of the cards and their uses became the blueprint for the secret society the Hermetic Order of the Golden Dawn.

Éliphas Lévi put the tarot at the centre of a system of magic, drawing a correspondence between each trump and the letters of the Hebrew alphabet

A TAROT TIMELINE

TAROT CROSSES THE CHANNEL
1861

English occultist Kenneth MacKenzie writes the *Cipher Manuscripts* after meeting with Éliphas Lévi. As British interest in the occult flourishes, it eventually inspires the founders of the Hermetic Order of the Golden Dawn.

THE BOOK OF DAYS
1864

Robert Chambers publishes *The Book of Days*, in which he examines the popularity of cartomancy amongst the wives of British soldiers. Chambers' interpretations of the cards prove influential with AE Waite, later to launch his own influential tarot deck.

THE GOLDEN DAWN
1888

William Westcott and Samuel Mathers form the Hermetic Order of the Golden Dawn. This British occult group follows the teaching of its own tarot, available only to its secretive membership list.

THE RIDER-WAITE DECK
1909

As the Golden Dawn splinters into different groups, member AE Waite seeks his own path through mysticism. In order to forge it, he employs illustrator Pamela Colman Smith to design what becomes the Rider-Waite tarot, a deck that takes its name from the author and his publisher, whilst downplaying the important role of the woman who drew it. Waite publishes a book, The Pictorial Key to the Tarot, to accompany the deck. Today, the Rider-Waite tarot is without a doubt the most recognisable deck still in popular use and the first deck of many a novice.

THE FOOL.

Into the occult

By the end of the 19th century, tarot cards had been adopted by those who sought to practice magic instead

When tarot cards first became popular in Europe, they were simple playthings, used to while away the hours enjoying a few games with friends. French cartomancers and mystics of the 18th century had taken them into new arenas, where a turn of a card could foretell the future. They had acquired multiple arcane meanings from sometimes questionable sources and the likes of the Tarot of Marseilles had been joined by custom-designed esoteric decks, each of which promised some new realm of understanding. Yet tarot had not yet finished its journey into the occult and, as the 19th century ticked down, they were about to enter perhaps their most notorious phase yet.

Éliphas Lévi had been the first practitioner to link tarot cards to ceremonial magic and his writings perfectly captured the spirit of the time. In the 1880s, it seemed as though Europe was in the grip of a fever for all things occult and mystical. Masonic lodges, esoteric societies and belief systems were springing up as people sought new outlets for their faith, or in which to practice rituals that the established church would never allow.

In 1861, Englishman Kenneth MacKenzie visited Éliphas Lévi in France for a discussion about his writings, his magical practices, and the deeper meanings that lay behind the tarot deck. The meeting with Lévi proved enormously influential for MacKenzie, and he returned to England brimming with ideas to establish his own lodge, which would run according to his own versions of Lévi's magical system. At the heart of the lodge's beliefs would be a brand new tarot deck of his own design. He produced reams of writing on the subject and central to it all were 60 cryptographic folios that constituted the *Cipher Manuscripts* and *Book T*, which purported to be based upon ancient manuscripts. In these books he laid out his vision for the Order of the Golden Dawn, and the teachings upon which it would be based.

In fact, Mackenzie didn't live to see out his dream. When he died, his papers were acquired by William Westcott and Samuel MacGregor Mathers. Together they decoded the *Cipher Manuscripts*, which offered exact details regarding the rituals and magical syllabus that the order should follow. Westcott and Mathers called in a fellow Freemason named William Woodman in order to

Samuel MacGregor Mathers, one of the founders of the Hermetic Order of the Golden Dawn, conducts a ceremony whilst wearing Egyptian regalia

> "In the 1880s it seemed as though Europe was in the grip of a fever for all things occult and mystical"

Lady Frieda Harris illustrated Aleister Crowley's Book of Thoth. At her encouragement, he reflected his own complex scientific, esoteric and astrological beliefs in the deck

convert the contents of the manuscript into a usable book, and the three established the first temple of the Hermetic Order of the Golden Dawn.

The Isis-Urania Temple was established in London in 1888. Unlike the Freemasons, it allowed women to join on an equal footing. Although Lévi had connected each of the trump cards to the Hebrew alphabet beginning with the Magician, the Order shifted each card's meaning by starting the correspondence between the alphabet and cards with the Fool. They replaced the King, Lévi's most powerful face card, with the Knight, and the Pages became Princesses. Each of the trumps had its place on the Tree of Life, and the members of the Order had their own secret deck.

The Golden Dawn tarot deck was based according to descriptions contained in *Book T*. It was likely initially drawn by Moina, the wife of Samuel Mathers, and it was not printed or published to anyone, even the members of the Order. Instead, members of the Hermetic Order of the Golden Dawn made their own hand-drawn tarot deck based on the original and coloured according to a strict guideline. Those who had yet to be fully admitted made do with hand-coloured versions of the Tarot de Marseilles instead.

From the Order of the Golden Dawn came AE Waite and Pamela Colman Smith. Together, they designed the Rider-Waite deck, which is arguably the most popular and famous deck to this day. The symbolism of these cards marked a departure from what had come before, particularly when it came to Christian imagery. Another significant change was the scenes that illustrated the pips, which had rarely had their own illustrations in past decks. Whilst the teachings of the Golden Dawn and Lévi were reflected in the deck, Waite made some significant changes to the order of the cards in order to better reflect his own belief in their system and meaning, changes that are still extant today.

The Golden Dawn had dissolved by 1903. As its members began to set up their own groups, one in particular emerged as particularly notorious. Aleister Crowley was one of the order's most notable former members. He has made a dramatic exit from the Golden Dawn in 1900 and quickly established his own orders so that he could follow his own path of "Magick". Frustrated by the tarot decks on offer, he sought an artist who could help him realise his own dreams and in 1937, was introduced to Lady Frieda Harris.

Lady Harris was the wife of Liberal Member of Parliament who was herself an enthusiast of the esoteric. It was she who encouraged Crowley to move away from traditional ideas about tarot and introduce his own particular brand of Magick to the illustrations. Over five years from 1939, she produced a series of oil paintings to illustrate Crowley's deck, the *Book of Thoth*. The Thoth reordered the astrological and Hebrew alphabet connections of each card, returning the order to that of the Tarot of Marseilles and included Crowley's own decades of occult scholarship. Though it remains a popular deck, it has been unable to unseat the Rider-Waite deck from its pedestal.

Modern tarot readers still use many of the older decks, but the world of tarot continues to innovate. Today, tarot readers can choose form a vast range of traditional and brand new decks, and techniques that range from Crowley's teachings to those of Waite and beyond. Tarot has not rested; instead, it continues to fascinate old and new enthusiasts alike.

From the Order of the Golden Dawn came AE Waite and Pamela Colman Smith

THE CLASSIC DECKS

Though innumerable tarot decks are available today, the legendary Tarot of Marseilles, Rider-Waite and Book of Thoth cards remain popular choices

For modern tarot readers, there is a seemingly endless selection of decks to choose from. There are tarot cards inspired by every aspect of life and interest you can think of from minimalist, feminist, Disney and cartoon decks to tarot cards devoted to cats, inspired by tattoo designs and illustrated by fine artists. Despite this, three classic decks remain as popular today as ever before and for many classic decks like the Tarot of Marseilles, the Rider-Waite and the Book of Thoth provide an ideal starting point to begin learning about the tarot, to deepen one's understanding of the cards or discover how to read them.

The Tarot of Marseilles is one of the oldest decks still in popular use and is believed to be the origin of modern European tarot. Its exact origins are lost to time, but it is believed that French soldiers first encountered tarot cards when they invaded Milan and the Piedmont in 1499. When they returned to France, they took with them examples of what was to become the Tarot of Marseilles. Its 78 cards and four suits, plus Major Arcana, are instantly recognisable to tarot readers today and, as the cards grew in popularity, new packs began to be produced from the original design. The oldest surviving pack using the original Marseilles illustrations was produced in Paris by Jean Noblet in around 1650. But it was in 1736 that a Marseilles-based printer named Chosson produced the grandfather of the modern deck. His designs were copied onto wood blocks in 1760 by Conver, and soon became the standard tarot across Europe.

As befits their origins in the 15th century, the playful designs of the Marseilles capture a medieval world of artisans, workers and monarchs. They did not, however, please everyone. Officials of the Catholic church took a dim view of cards such as the Pope and Papesse, which depicts a controversial female pope, and even forced some manufacturers to substitute these cards with replacements that had no ecclesiastical element. Yet this had little impact on the swift proliferation of the Marseilles and its influence. As the decks spread across the continent, regions often made alterations of their own to reflect

THE VISCONTI-SFORZA TAROT

The Visconti-Sforza Tarot is a collection of over a dozen incomplete 15th century decks, which are the oldest surviving decks in the world. They come from an era when tarot was referred to as Trinofi, meaning triumph, and they were employed not for divination, but games.

The decks were commissioned initially by Filippo Maria Visconti, Duke of Milan, and then by his son-in-law, Francesco Sforza, and they are ornate works of art. Created as they were at the height of the Renaissance, they are richly detailed and decorated and their imagery is strongly reminiscent of the world that the Visconti knew so well. They conform mostly to the model we know today, though the apparent number of cards in each deck can vary as well as some of the names of the cards, but we can easily recognise the Major and Minor Arcana, and four suits of bastoni, cups, spades and denari.

The influence of the Visconti-Sforza can be seen in the decks that followed it and those that are used today. Although none of the decks are complete, when they have been reissued, attempts have been made to illustrate replacements for those lost, in the style of the original works.

Opulent, richly detailed and filled with symbolism, these cards are unmistakably a product of Renaissance Italy

"Two members of the Hermetic Order of the Golden Dawn went on to create the most famous tarot deck of all"

local sentiments or sensitivities. During the French Revolution, the Emperor and Empress were replaced by cards representing the Grandmother and Grandfather, whilst in Turin the animal dogging the heels of the Fool was replaced by a butterfly in front of him.

When the Marseilles returned to its origins in Italy, printers and artists initially reprinted the deck as it was. Over time, however, they began to make subtle changes to the designs. They added double headed characters, much like those on playing cards, and went to town on designing others. Previously sombre court cards now gained bright costumes and animated expressions, whilst pip cards were embellished with all the artistry of an illuminated manuscript. Though easily identifiable when placed against their fellow cards from the Marseilles deck, there is no mistaking later Italian efforts.

The Tarot de Marseilles had been a popular choice for the game of tarot, but as the years passed new fashions emerged. Animal tarots, many of which have been lost, became popular throughout Europe. These incorporated illustrations of animals into the imagery and added characters recognisable from folk tales or similar sources. Amongst these was the popular Bavarian Animal Tarot and its successor the Belgian Animal Tarot, which became particularly dominant and remained in production into the late 19th century.

Just as design tastes moved on, so did the fickle needs of card players. When they switched away from tarot cards to tarock decks for gaming, the future looked bleak. Instead, those who preferred to use tarot for divination rather than playing games adopted it as their own. 18th century French tarot occultists saved the Tarot de Marseilles from being consigned to the history books as a medieval curiosity, and word of their enthusiasm for tarot soon spread across the English Channel.

The Hermetic Order of the Golden Dawn was created in the United Kingdom in 1886. This esoteric lodge was based upon the writings of the late Kenneth MacKenzie, an occultist who hoped to establish a new set of teachings based around a tarot deck. Though this deck was hand-drawn and distributed only to members of the group, two members of the Hermetic Order of the Golden Dawn went on to create the most famous tarot deck of all.

In 1909 writer AE Waite found himself at a crossroads of belief, torn between the Golden Dawn's emphasis on ceremony and his own mystic beliefs. In an effort to popularise his

Designed by the notorious occultist Aleister Crowley, the Book of Thoth has long been associated with Crowley's own brand of ceremonial magick

way of thinking he formed the Fellowship of the Rosy Cross which, like the Golden Dawn, would use a tarot deck as the key to its beliefs. Waite conceived the deck as a series of archetypal images that would offer users a portal through which to connect with the divine. He employed fellow member of the Golden Dawn, Pamela Colman Smith, to draw the cards, many of which show inspiration from the Marseilles, whilst others clearly display the influence of the 15th century Sola Busca tarot deck, albeit adapted to Smith's own artistic sensibilities.

Waite wrote a book entitled *The Pictorial Key to Tarot* to accompany the deck and it has remained the best-selling deck ever since. Bright, accessible and easy to adapt to all manner of belief systems and approaches, it is frequently the choice of the beginner. Sadly, whilst Waite and the publishing house that created the deck gave their names to the Rider-Waite deck, Smith's contribution was brushed aside. Today, many tarot practitioners refer to this deck as the Rider-Waite-Smith, in an effort to recognise the enormous contribution of Pamela Colman Smith.

One person who could not be accused of being brushed out of the history of his deck is infamous occultist Aleister Crowley. Crowley is perhaps the most famous practitioner of the 20th century, and his devotion to mysticism has been both vilified and venerated. The *Book of Thoth*, as Crowley named his deck and the book that accompanied it, was intended to create a deck specifically tailored to Crowley's magical needs, and it would incorporate everything from science to philosophy to ancient occultism, with the overarching emphasis on what Crowley referred to as Magick.

The Art Deco designs of the Thoth were created by Lady Freida Harris, who produced oil paintings for the cards according to Crowley's concepts. Crowley renamed some of the cards, such as Strength and Temperance, which became Lust and Art, and though his deck certainly takes elements from the Golden Dawn's own tarot, it is very much an expression of its creator's interests. By the time the deck was completed in 1943 however, the Rider-Waite had secured its footing as the tarot pack that dominated all others.

Just as some tarot practitioners constantly redesigned the cards for their own uses, tarot has evolved through the centuries and continues to do so. It has adapted through Crowley's Magick and beyond, becoming a staple of New Age practice with examples such as the 1991 Arthurian Tarot. Designed around the legends of King Arthur, the deck updates the suits to fit the theme, placing Spears, Swords, Stones and Grails in a deck typified not by Major and Minor Arcana but by Greater and Lesser powers. With a strong Celtic influence, this work by Caitlin and John Matthews continues to be a popular choice today. Likewise, the esoteric blending of influences favoured by the likes of Crowley can be seen in examples such as Suzanne Treister's visually dazzling Hexen 2.0, or the vintage monochromatic collage of Sarah Ovenall's Victoria Regina Tarot. There are also tarot-adjacent products often known as oracle cards. These don't contain the typical suits, court cards and Major Arcana of the traditional tarot but instead a collection of archetypal imagery, often drawn from mythology or folklore, that forms a series of prompts for meditation and spiritual guidance.

Tarot has always been an evolving form of art, divination and teaching. Today it continues to capture the imagination of new readers, whether in one of the classic decks or a newly-imaged set of cards. With innumerable decks to choose from featuring everything from original woodcuts to arcane mysticism and brightly coloured, instantly accessible modern imagery, this feast of visual treats and meaning offers something for every taste.

When AE White found himself at a crossroads of belief, he employed Pamela Colman Smith to illustrate what has become the world's most famous tarot deck

As an influential member of the Hermetic Order of the Golden Dawn, Crowley found that even the most arcane decks simply didn't meet his needs

The Book of Thoth was specifically tailored to Aleister Crowley's magical needs

THE
CARDS

Exploring tarot's unique imagery
and the meanings of the cards

THE
MAJOR
ARCANA

The tarot's trump cards are symbolic archetypes and divinatory devices that contain mystical meanings and express a philosophical journey when laid out sequentially

The Major Arcana cards can be interpreted, when placed in numeric order, as an allegory of the human journey into higher consciousness

> The Major Arcana narrates an allegorical tale known as The Fool's Journey

THE SUN.

WHEEL of FORTUNE.

The Major Arcana are the named and numbered trump cards in a pack of tarot cards. These cards always overpower the other cards in both impact and outcome and indicate important events. In the Rider-Waite-Coleman deck there are 22 cards in the Major Arcana, all numbered in Roman numerals except that of the Fool, who is given the number zero. In other decks, the Fool is often un-numbered completely or placed after the trump cards. When reading tarot, the Major Arcana trump all other cards pulled, and should be interpreted as the most significant. Their importance also increases as you follow the sequence from I to XXI.

THE ORDER OF THE MAJOR ARCANA

In the Rider-Waite tarot, the trump cards are: The Fool (0), The Magician (I), The High Priestess (II), The Empress (III), The Emperor (IV), The Hierophant (V), The Lovers (VI) , The Chariot (VII), Strength (VIII), The Hermit (IX), The Wheel Of Fortune (X), Justice (XI), The Hanged Man (XII), Death (XIII), Temperance (XIV), The Devil (XV), The Tower (XVI), The Star (XVII), The Moon (XVII), The Sun (XIX), Judgement (XX) and The World (XXI).

> **"With each repetition of the journey, The Fool reaches a new, higher level of understanding and consciousness"**

In older decks such as the Tarot de Marseilles, Court de Gébelin and Etteilla's Tarot, the Strength and Justice cards are the other way around. These were altered by the Hermetic Order of the Golden Dawn (of which both Arthur Edward Waite and Pamela Colman Smith were members) in accordance with the order of their astrological correspondences. These are as follows: Air (The Fool), Mercury, the Moon, Venus, Aries, Taurus, Gemini, Cancer, Leo, Virgo, Jupiter, Libra, Water, Scorpio, Sagittarius, Capricorn, Mars, Aquarius, Pisces, the Sun, Fire, and Saturn.

THE FOOL'S JOURNEY

The Major Arcana can be read as an allegory, dubbed 'The Fool's Journey', believed to represent the stages of life and an initiatory sequence of events that establishes a human's path of spiritual ascension, or self-discovery, and the challenges we face along this path. Each trump card represents an archetype, challenge, obstacle, lesson or reward along life's path, and they can all be compiled into three groups of seven cards, each representing a different stage of life that forces a person to grow. The Fool, who does not have a Roman numeral assigned to it, represents the everyday human, who journeys through each of the trump cards in order. However, the fool never ends the journey, repeating it over and over and growing each time, interacting with each card on a higher spiritual and self-aware level.

STAGE ONE

The first act begins with the Fool card, representing the basic human archetype, a simple, innocent soul who is open and ready to begin their first part of their spiritual ascent, through personal lessons and growth. Cards I to VII represent various aspects of day-to-day life and the social realm, asking questions about identity and relationships with others and the wants and needs of humanity. The Magician and High Priestess represent both conscious and unconscious awareness, willpower, unrealised potential and intuition. The Emperor and the Empress are the mother and father archetypes, and our introduction to nature and sensuality, and structure and authority. The Hierophant is the world of conforming, organised belief systems and education. The Lovers are sexual awakening, relationships and values, and finally, the Chariot is maturation, the sense of a strong identity and the confidence, occasional arrogance, of youth.

STAGE TWO

The second act of ascension is where the Fool begins to look further afield and learn about time, morality and virtue

The Fool, or jester, was often used as a representation of the everyman. Here he is shown performing the danse macabre, an allegory of the universality of death that dates back to medieval times

– or the will of humanity. Strength offers the quiet courage to continue despite setbacks, patience and tolerance. The Hermit forces the Fool to look inwards, to ask why and search for a deeper truth and to seek solitude, following their own path. The Wheel Of Fortune is a symbol of the mysterious yet harmonious universe, pushing the Fool to recognise their part in this world, embrace change and to act towards their destiny and purpose. Justice is the act of taking responsibility for your actions, and a time of big decisions, while the Hanged Man forces The Fool to let go, to be open and vulnerable and surrender to their experiences, embracing obstacles to fulfil their goal. Death is the changes the Fool makes to themselves, ending things that no longer serve them in order to transition into a more fulfilling way of life – often interpreted as the death of the ego – and Temperance is the balance that the Fool has found since embracing themselves: stable, centred and harmonious.

STAGE THREE

The third act begins with the bad (the Devil) and ends with the good (the World). It is the final ascent towards a higher spiritual power, reason, absolute understanding and godliness. After finding a level of fulfilment in life, the Devil represents the material seductions that may lead us off our path, or things that the Fool may still be holding on to that are preventing him from achieving true enlightenment. The Tower frees the Fool from the grasp of the Devil with sudden painful change, release and revelation. Following this monumental shift, the Star offers hope and inspiration once again. The peace after the storm. The Moon is a time to rest and prepare, another time of reflection and once again shedding anything holding the Fool back, perhaps aspects of the Jungian "shadow self" or fears and anxieties that once again need to be addressed. The Sun symbolises the victory over those shadows, the Fool's inner light, pure radiance and joy. Judgement is the Fool's readiness to ascend into a higher level of consciousness, having finally understood their purpose, free of ego. Finally, the World is the end of the cycle, yet also a new beginning. The Fool is accomplished, fulfilled and ready to re-enter the world with a new level of understanding. With each repetition, The Fool reaches a higher level of understanding and consciousness.

The Fool is shown walking towards a precipice, unaware of the dangers which lie in wait for him

THE FOOL .

The Fool represents us all as we set out unprepared on the journey through life

When the Fool beats people around the head it reflects his role in puncturing our own pretensions

THE
FOOL
A FREE SPIRIT

There is an innocence embodied by The Fool, but there can be dangers to ignoring hard realities

The Major Arcana starts with The Fool. This is appropriate as he embodies the journey that everyone must take through life. We start as innocents with the world at our feet but sometimes, like the Fool standing on a cliff edge, our lack of knowledge can lead us into danger. Some interpretations of the Major Arcana frame them as 'The Fool's Journey.' Only by passing through all the steps they represent does a person come to a full understanding of themselves and the universe.

The Fool in the upright position signifies all the opportunities that are just waiting for us to grasp. New beginnings often start with us completely unaware of the challenges that await. Yet this can be a strength. If we all knew the difficulties a project would entail along the way, many of us would never start. The Fool encourages us to take on new things with an open heart and to also throw caution to the wind.

When presented with the Fool it may be that you need to unleash your inner child. What is it you want? What is the first step you need to take to reach it? Often the biggest hurdle in a venture is casting off our self doubt. The Fool has no doubt. Act now.

The other side of the Fool comes when it is reversed. Sometimes a person blinds themselves to the potential risk of a course of action. Are you being heedless? The Fool warns of the dangers of that. A leap of faith is fine, but sometimes you do need to look where you leap.

Even in its reversed position, however, the Fool can still be a prompt to take action. It can mean that your need to have control over every facet of your life is holding you back. This card points towards a need for balance between considering every step and just jumping straight in.

THE FOOL

NUMBER: 0

·

CARD
A young man dressed as a jester stands on the edge of a precipice with a traveller's bundle on his back, unaware of the fall in front of him.

·

UPRIGHT
Innocence, opportunities, potential. Take a leap of faith.

REVERSED
Unreadiness, fear of the unknown, recklessness. Look before you leap.

> "The Fool in the upright position signifies all the opportunities that are just waiting for us to grasp"

I

On a table in front of the Magician are a cup, a sword, a wand, and a pentacle – the four suits of the Minor Arcana

THE MAGICIAN.

The power of the Magician can be shown through his ability to convince his audience of his arcane knowledge

The Magician is sometimes known as Le Bateleur

THE — MAGICIAN
POWER AND POTENTIAL

The Magician is the master of the esoteric arts who is able to get what he wants, but also the master of illusions

In the most popular illustration of the Magician, he is shown with all of the symbols of the Minor Arcana before him. These four objects also represent the four classical elements of earth, air, fire, and water. He has learned from the hidden arts how to control all of these things. How? His hands point the way. One points towards the heavens and one points down to the ground. As above, so below. He has realised the power of connections and is in full control of his talents.

When the Magician appears in the upright position, he is a representation of the ability to bring our desires and willpower out into the world. What the mind wants the body is able to produce. Again, as above, so below. When this card is drawn it can be a sign that now is the time to act. All is ready for you to put your efforts into effect and make what you want to happen a reality.

That is not to say that the Magician is a call to act rashly. Careful study is required to achieve his mastery in magic, and this card is letting you know that your preparations are on the right course. If you are working towards something, keep going and know that your talents will get you through.

When the Magician is reversed, however, it is a warning that you are being tricked, either by yourself or someone else. Le Bateleur, as this card is sometimes called, is a confidence trickster that exploits people's credulity. Are you being manipulated in some way?

The reversed Magician can also mean that you are wasting your talents. Do you have something that you wish to do that you feel unworthy to try? Until you give yourself the confidence you will never give it a go. It can also be a sign that your are aiming at the wrong thing. Do you want power for its own sake or do you really want to make things better?

THE MAGICIAN

NUMBER: 1

CARD
A man stands with one hand raised, holding a wand, and the other pointed towards the ground. Before him on a table stand a pentacle, a cup, a sword, and a wand.

UPRIGHT
Power, resourcefulness, skill. Remember you are powerful.

REVERSED
Lack of planning, manipulation, wasted talents. Are you being tricked?

> "He is a representation of the ability to bring our desires and willpower out into the world"

THE HIGH PRIESTESS

INTUITION

The High Priestess signifies that sometimes you need to listen to what your intuition is telling you

THE HIGH PRIESTESS

NUMBER: 2

CARD
A young woman wearing a crown sits between a black and a white pillar. A scroll rests in her hand. Beneath her foot is a crescent moon.

UPRIGHT
Intuition, hidden knowledge, the subconscious. Trust your gut.

REVERSED
Uncertainty, secrets, conceit. Get out into the world.

The High Priestess sits in a place of authority, but not merely over this world. Her crown, sometimes a papal tiara, points to hers being a spiritual leadership. In many cards, she is shown in the rich blue cloak of the Virgin Mary. In others she rests her feet on the crescent moon, which has long been a symbol of sacred knowledge. The curtain behind her points to the hidden realms of wisdom which she has access to.

When the High Priestess is drawn in the upright position she is a teacher – but one which tells us to listen to our hearts. Hers is the knowledge of the inner spirit. This most often manifests in intuition. Our gut tells us whether something is right or wrong. The appearance of the High Priestess can be a sign to fully trust yourself and the things you have planned. Conversely, the High Priestess could mean that further meditation is necessary to understand what it is you truly want. The answer that you seek to a problem will come from within.

Ignoring the outer world and becoming obsessed with what is going on in your own mind can be dangerous. This one of the reasons a person may draw the High Priestess in the reversed position. By paying too much attention to ourselves, we risk losing contact with reality. This card can be a warning that we need to rebalance our conscious and subconscious.

The reversed High Priestess can point towards secrets that have been held inside for too long. Sometimes truths need to be spoken even when we fear the outcome. It may be that a problem needs to be viewed from both your internal point of view and that of others.

There is both wisdom that comes from within and without.

> **"The appearance of the High Priestess can be a sign to fully trust yourself and the things you have planned"**

Some versions of the tarot call this card 'The Popess' and show her in the regalia of a Pope

The veil behind the High Priestess represents the thin barrier between the conscious and unconscious mind

The papal tiara underlines the High Priestess' power, while the open book she holds represents the access she has to knowledge

THE HIGH PRIESTESS

THE EMPRESS
CARD OF NURTURE

The Empress is not only beautiful – she holds all
the power of nature in her hands

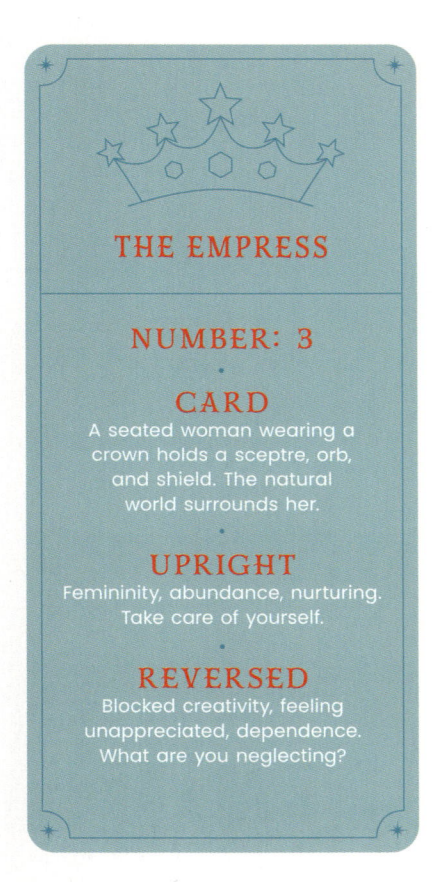

THE EMPRESS

NUMBER: 3

CARD
A seated woman wearing a
crown holds a sceptre, orb,
and shield. The natural
world surrounds her.

UPRIGHT
Femininity, abundance, nurturing.
Take care of yourself.

REVERSED
Blocked creativity, feeling
unappreciated, dependence.
What are you neglecting?

The Empress represents all that may be achieved in this world. The ripening crops which often surround her throne show plans and possibilities coming to fruition. Above all, the Empress is the rejuvenating power of nature. As a woman in power, she brings all of the gifts that have traditionally been associated with femininity: fertility, nurture, and creativity.

The Empress card in the upright position can be a simple reminder of all the gifts that have been given to you. It tells you to appreciate all that surrounds you and the opportunities you have for growth. Some versions of the Empress underline her fertility by showing her as pregnant. This can mean that a literal pregnancy is coming or that a fresh chance in life is on the way.

If you have responsibility for others then the Empress is calling you to take a nurturing approach to your dealings with them. Gentleness and a soft hand may yield results where strictness fails. The bounty of nature reminds us that there is plenty of kindness to go around. The Empress is a card of forgiveness and the start of a new cycle.

When the Empress is reversed it tells a person that they need to offer some love and attention to themselves. It is impossible to nurture others if you are not also caring for yourself. If an unhealthy dependence has formed then this card is a reminder to set boundaries in your personal relationships. Are you taking a motherly role too far? Sometimes you need to release something for it to grow. The Reversed Empress also suggests that your mind is blocked in some way. Is there an idea, dream, or desire that you are struggling to give birth to?

The Empress is a call for you to trust in your best nature. Being supportive of others will in turn win support for you, but you must also support yourself.

> **"When the Empress is reversed it tells a person that they need to offer some love and attention to themselves"**

The Empress sits on a throne surrounded by the abundant bounty of nature that suggest the fruitful powers of creation

The Empress is often shown enthroned, crowned, and holding a shield to represent the power that she wields

A starry crown connects the Empress to the heavens and the cycles of nature, and her sovereignty over them

THE EMPRESS.

The Emperor is shown in armour and crowned – he is a person in full power just as fate may hold us in its grip

The Emperor holds an orb, representing the world, in his hand. The whole world can fall under the sway of authority and tradition

Some tarot sets show the Emperor holding an ankh sign, but sometimes he grasps a simple mace to display his power

THE EMPEROR.

THE — EMPEROR

AUTHORITY

The Emperor is a strategic thinker who represents strength and stability

The Emperor is the paternal figure of the tarot and represents many of those things a father has traditionally been. He is a supporter but also a strict person. He offers stability but may also control those around him. Where there is tradition there can also be a lack of freedom. Beyond the mere familial role, this card shows a man with all the trappings of temporal power. He holds a sceptre and orb, is garbed in armour, and wears a crown.

When the Emperor is drawn in the upright position it can mean that great things are coming your way. It may be that you are called on to lead in your personal life or in your work. When the responsibility comes your way, you will act like a good father who protects and nurtures those he holds dear.

The Emperor is often a centre of calm. This card may be telling you to play a similar role. You will set the rules and examples which will help others to become their best selves. This card can be pointing towards a need to follow the traditions you have created and keep to the path you have set.

If the Emperor is reversed it can be read as a dereliction of duty. Is there an aspect of your life you know you should be attending to but are not? It may be that you are acting like the bad father who judges harshly and offers no kindness. Perhaps you are not behaving maturely. It could also be that you are thinking too rigidly and not allowing yourself the flexibility to change and grow. Even when reversed the Emperor can be a positive card. One of the marks of a good ruler is benevolence. You may find an opportunity to forgive another person, or you may need a little clemency yourself.

The Emperor tells us to get control of ourselves and take responsibility.

THE EMPEROR

NUMBER: 4

·

CARD
A wise old man with a long beard is crowned and sitting on a stone throne. Behind him looms a barren mountain range.

·

UPRIGHT
Tradition, authority, stability. Prepare to take control.

·

REVERSED
Rigidity, domination, lack of control. Don't be afraid to break free!

> "Beyond the mere familial role this card shows a man with all the trappings of temporal power"

The Hierophant is a religious figure that helps to bridge the realms of the human and the divine

The Hierophant is sometimes called the Pope, or Teacher of Wisdom, but he always embodies spirituality

The blessing hand gesture used by the Hierophant shows two fingers pointing up towards heaven

V

THE HIEROPHANT

5 LE PAPE

IL PAPA

THE HIEROPHANT
TRADITION AND BELIEFS

The spiritual guidance offered by the Hierophant helps us know when to conform and when to break free

The Hierophant, which means a person who interprets sacred mysteries, is often shown in papal regalia. This is fitting as this card represents the original meaning of pontiff – 'bridge-builder.' The Hierophant is the one who helps to guide people between the mundane and spiritual spheres. He is sometimes depicted between two pillars which stand for liberty and law. It is the Hierophant who explains when to follow tradition and when to act for yourself. Those who kneel before him are accepting his spiritual wisdom.

When the Hierophant is in the upright position, it means that a traditional, orthodox approach is needed at this time. A well-placed plan can help you achieve your goals. Holding on to the status quo at this time could be the best course of action. It may also suggest that you have to consult your moral compass and follow what is right.

Just as the Hierophant is the teacher of wisdom, when this card is drawn it might be pointing you towards a role of leadership. Someone must take charge of a situation. Ask yourself whether that person is you. If you decide that now is not your moment then the Hierophant can be advising you to pay heed to someone whose wisdom you trust. Consult others who may be able to help.

Sometimes what needs to be done is not what we have always done. When the Hierophant is in the reversed position it signals that a new strategy is required. It is time to break free from the rules that may be constricting you. The reversed Hierophant is an agent of non-conformity.

Yet, there is a risk to forging your own path. The reversed Hierophant can also be a warning. Are you abandoning your beliefs? Are you ignoring the past lessons and tradition unnecessarily? Learning to balance freedom and structure is truly the heart of wisdom.

THE HIEROPHANT

NUMBER: 5

CARD
A man in religious regalia sits on a throne and makes a gesture of blessing with his hand. Keys at his feet hint to him unlocking secrets.

UPRIGHT
Wisdom, spirituality, tradition. Follow the path before you.

REVERSED
Freedom, rule breaking, personal beliefs. Take an unorthodox approach.

> "The Hierophant is the one who helps guide people between the mundane and spiritual spheres"

THE LOVERS

A DUALITY

The Lovers is not just a card about romance – it can signify any number of relationships that are important

THE LOVERS

NUMBER: 6

·

CARD

A naked man and woman stand underneath a watching angel. Behind them a serpent coils among the branches of the Tree of Good and Evil.

·

UPRIGHT

Love, relationships, choices. Trust your heart.

·

REVERSED

Disharmony, distrust, imbalance. What do you really want?

Love has always been slightly mysterious. In ancient myth, it was caused by the love arrows of Eros, which seemed to fall on people randomly. There is no accounting for taste. In some versions of the Lovers. this unruly passion is shown blindly shooting his arrows. In one of the most popular tarot decks, the Lovers are depicted as Adam and Eve in the Garden of Eden. In their nudity they conceal nothing from each other, but a snake lurks menacingly behind them. Love can cause the greatest happiness and the greatest grief – this card holds that duality.

When the Lovers is drawn in its upright position it can signify that you have made the right choice in your partner. All is going well and will continue to do so. This card is about more than just romance or sex. It could mean that a platonic or familial relation is well-balanced and filled with open communication. The man and woman coming together as lovers represents two forces, almost opposites, being united in something greater than either.

Although unexpected people may fall in love or become friends, this card also deals in choices. Though it may not seem like it, we always have choices. To stay with a partner or friend is a choice. This card may be telling you to stick with them through a hard time.

When the card is reversed it could be pointing to a division between you and a loved one. What was once a partnership has become unbalanced. It can also reveal that a tough choice is coming. Give the options you are considering just as much thought as you would choosing a lover.

Love can be a life-long commitment. The Lovers always reminds us that there are consequences to all of our choices. Before you reach your decision be sure that you can handle the outcome.

> "Love can cause the greatest happiness and the greatest grief - this card holds that duality"

Sometimes the Lovers are shown being struck by the arrow of love, shot by an angel wearing a blindfold

L'AMOUREUX

Although love can strike at any time, this card may serve as a warning to be cautious in who choose as your partner

In some versions, the Lovers are depicted as Adam and Eve, the first lovers, to represent lost innocence

THE LOVERS.

THE CHARIOT
DETERMINATION

The seventh card of the Major Arcana is an active card that suggests victory through perseverance and mastering control

THE CHARIOT

NUMBER: 7

CARD
A man stands on a chariot drawn by two sphinxes – light and dark. He carries a sword, staff or wand, and above him is a curtain adorned with stars. On the chariot is a shield with a spinning top image inside it that is surmounted by the solar disk and wings of Horus.

UPRIGHT
Confidence, determination, perseverance, victory, control over opposing forces, travel, preparation.

REVERSED
Lack of direction, unbalanced energies, self-doubt, feelings of being stuck or trapped, lack of drive, defeat.

The Chariot is a card of triumph, depicting a prince, king or warrior who wields a sword, according to AE Waite, although Coleman illustrates it with a staff or sceptre, and it bears both a sword and sceptre in the Tarot of Marseilles. This isn't a victorious warrior returning from battle, however; he is on the first stretch of his journey, parading through the streets to set out on his fated path. The star-covered canopy above his head is a reminder of the fates and the universe.

In the Rider–Waite deck, he is pulled by two sphinxes, one light and one dark, but to proceed, he must overcome their riddles and pull together their two opposing forces to achieve balance and control. Upon each of his shoulders are Urim and Thummim – divinatory tools used by Israeli priests. His skirt is covered in runic hieroglyphs or alchemical symbols. He has many tools at his fingertips but which will be chosen? Which will he master to move forward? The winged sun disc set in the shield at the front of his chariot shows the top part of the Greek messenger god Hermes' staff, the Caduceus. A sun with wings, it is an alchemical symbol and signifies divine power or royalty. It is at the very helm of the Chariot, indicating flight or movement towards the sun. Victory will be had if the aspiring hero is able to wield and control his chariot successfully.

The charioteer sits in a square chariot with a square upon his chest, further signifying that he represents control through preparation, readiness and mastery. His chariot, however, means that he maintains a link to the physical world. He needs it in order to move forward towards his fate. He is not yet ready to leave it behind. The spinning-top shape within the shield on the front of the Chariot is a modified Hindu Yoni-Lingam symbol, a tantric representation of sex, indicating that the charioteer has moved past his more immature relationship with sexual desire and has grown into a mature adult, able to control his primal needs and impulses. But even if interpreted as simply a spinning top, it still indicates finding balance in order to achieve success.

The outcome of the card is a positive one, whichever direction you move in and tackle, or obstacles you face, you will prevail with willpower. However, the chariot could be toppled without delicate control, indicating a need for balance, stability and momentum.

> ❝Whichever direction you move in or obstacles you face, you will prevail❞

The modified Yoni-Lingam tantric sex symbol is depicted on the Chariot's coat of arms

LE CHARIOT

The Egyptian winged sun disc was a symbol of divinity and power, and formed the head of the Greek god Hermes' (Mercury in Roman mythology) staff, the Caduceus, which was depicted as having two snakes entwined or copulating around it

Like the Marseilles Tarot, the Tarot of Piedmont's chariot is horse-drawn

THE CHARIOT.

The symbol of infinity appears above the head of the woman on the Strength card, representing a number which is boundless or endless, larger than any other

VIII

STRENGTH.

The Strength card of the Charles VI Tarot (also known as the Estensi or Gringonneur Tarot, of which only 17 cards remain and majority of which are on display at the Bibliotheque Nationale in Paris) features no lion, but a female capable of breaking, or perhaps fixing, columns

The Marseilles Strength card may have derived from the 15th century Cary-Yale Visconti-Sforza Tarot

STRENGTH

CONTROLLED POWER

The Strength card denotes strength of conviction through tamed reaction and influence without aggression

Historically named Fortitude, the Strength card was swapped in order with Justice, in accordance with the Golden Dawn's astrological sequence, to make it the eighth card, rather than the 11th. As such, the card is associated with the astrological sign of Leo, the sign represented by the lion and associated with traits such as confidence, passion, drama and dominance.

The woman featured in the Rider-Waite tarot shows calm and gentle dominance over the lion and, just like the Magician, has the symbol of life (or infinity) suspended over her head, linking the two cards and indicating an infinite amount of power is wielded by both. The two cards also share another commonality: roses. Roses represent masculine energies, but when adorning the women, they simply highlight that this is a more demure form of strength, rather than one of pure physical power.

The woman is dressed in white, a symbol of purity, while the lion is red, symbolising passion or rage. The chain of flowers indicates gentle force, but a force that is still capable of restraining a mighty beast. This card represents calm, controlled, assertive strength rather than aggression. Strength through mental and spiritual means and not just physical brawn. The woman's control over the lion, with no need to wrestle the animal, also suggests a moral strength and power over lust, passion and desires that are represented by the lion.

The lion is submissive, as indicated by it licking the woman's hand. This could also show that the animal not only recognises the woman's dominance, but also her compassion, and it is reciprocating it. Therefore, showing compassion while asserting a strength of character will be met with similar understanding. As both the lion and the woman are connected via the floral chain, they have achieved a harmonious relationship in which they both exist as one, despite the woman being in control of the animal – or in control of her own animalistic nature – there is a feeling of tranquillity.

STRENGTH

NUMBER: 8

·

CARD
A woman dressed in white, with a crown of flowers and an infinity sign above her head, closes the jaws of a lion. A chain of flowers binds them as the lion licks her hand.

·

UPRIGHT
Determination, strength of mind and character, control, confidence, compassion, persuasion and influence.

·

REVERSED
Hedonism, lack of courage, weakness, uncontrolled emotion, vulnerability.

> "The animal not only recognises the woman's dominance, but her compassion"

IX

THE HERMIT.

The Rider–Waite–Smith Hermit card as illustrated by Pamela Colman Smith and published in 1909

An earlier version of the Hermit tarot card, taken from the 15th Century Charles VI or Gringonneur Deck, showing him holding an hourglass instead of a lamp

A late-medieval depiction of St Christopher carrying Christ, with a Christian hermit holding up a lantern to guide them

THE HERMIT
LIGHTING THE WAY

Pause for reflection and contemplation and you will shine brighter and as a guiding light

Earlier interpretations of the Hermit have him holding an hourglass, representing fate and the passage of time. He is often compared to the Roman god Saturn, who was associated with fate and death until the late 15th century, when the Renaissance re-shaped him into a god of contemplation and artistic genius.

Historically, hermits were solitary Christian monks; as such they wandered the desert practising abstinence and living an ascetic life, focused on withdrawing from society and devoting themselves to God. The Hermit in the Rider-Waite tarot, therefore, symbolises inward thought and devotion. He is isolated from society, high above on a mountaintop, and holds a lantern, seeking knowledge closer to the heavens. Within the Hermit's lantern is a star, representing calm clarity, light and truth. He also shares elements with an image in AE Waite's Hermetic Museum – a female, robed alchemist who holds a six-point star. Alchemists aimed to change base metals into precious metals, and the Hermit is an alchemist of sorts. He has the ability to change his own base human form into a divine being and gain infinite wisdom if he is able to pause and withdraw himself (indicated by the Hermit's gaze being focused upon the ground), sacrifice material objects and/or superficial thoughts, meditate, reassess and contemplate.

While he separates himself from the material and physical restraints of society, he does not remain a lone wanderer. Neither does he wander without purpose. The lantern being held out in front indicates that he is a pioneer and truth-seeker, forging his own path rather than following others and, most importantly, lighting the way for those who also seek enlightenment to follow behind him. According to Waite, "His beacon intimates that 'where I am, you also may be'." The Hermit's staff represents his authority, strength and wisdom gained from his ability to remove all distractions and look deep inside himself. From his experience, he is able to inspire and teach others how they can do the same.

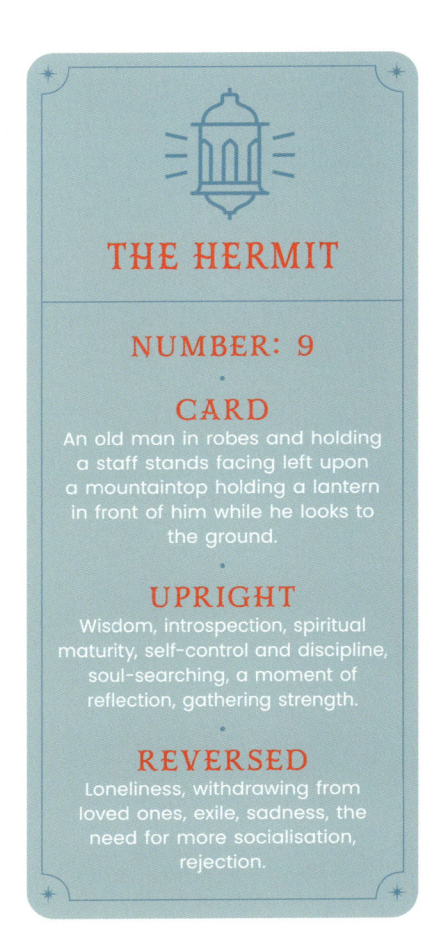

THE HERMIT

NUMBER: 9

CARD
An old man in robes and holding a staff stands facing left upon a mountaintop holding a lantern in front of him while he looks to the ground.

UPRIGHT
Wisdom, introspection, spiritual maturity, self-control and discipline, soul-searching, a moment of reflection, gathering strength.

REVERSED
Loneliness, withdrawing from loved ones, exile, sadness, the need for more socialisation, rejection.

> "He is a pioneer and truth-seeker, forging his own path rather than following others"

THE WHEEL OF FORTUNE

THE CYCLE OF FATE

What goes around comes around with the Wheel Of Fortune. Your destiny is already in motion

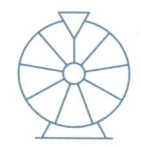

THE WHEEL OF FORTUNE

NUMBER: 10

CARD
The wheel adorned with symbols. On the top sits a sphinx, below is a jackal-headed man, to the left is a snake. In each corner of the card are winged animals: A human, eagle, lion and ox.

UPRIGHT
Abundance and fertility, change for the better, authority, virility, good things are in motion, luck, destiny.

REVERSED
Bad luck, misfortune, delays, setbacks.

The poet and mystic AE Waite based his Wheel of Fortune on French occultist Éliphas Lévi's card, as he did with many of the Rider-Waite trumps. "The symbolic picture stands for the perpetual motion of the fluidic universe and for the flux of human life," he wrote in his Pictorial Key To The Tarot.

Sat on the wheel is the sphinx, representing "the equilibrium therein", it holds an upright sword, representing virtue, power and mercy. In each corner of the card are the biblical creatures of Ezekiel, from top-left to bottom-left clockwise, they are the man, eagle, lion and ox. They can also all be associated with the zodiac, from top-left, clockwise: Aquarius, Scorpio, Leo and Taurus. On the wheel, the letters placed upon the cardinal directions can spell out ROTA when read from the bottom (Latin for wheel), or TARO when read from the top. Between these letters are Hebrew letters that spell the name of God.

There is an alchemical dial within the wheel, with the symbol for mercury to the north, sulphur to the east, dissolution to the south and salt to the west. These are the processes a human must go through in order to achieve enlightenment. Mercury is associated with the female, but also the snake and the mind that transcends death. Sulphur is brimstone, heat and masculinity, and also the soul. Dissolution is a process of transformation, dissolving the ego and achieving freedom. Salt represents the body and physical matter in its initial state, it needs to be dissolved and purified. Below the wheel is Hermanubis, a combination of the Egyptian god Anubis and the Greek god Hermes, a guiding soul representing good. To the left is the Greek god Typhon in his serpent form, symbolising evil.

This is a card of impermanence and good fortune. Allow the universe to guide you and the better your outcome will be. The good god is rising, while the bad is descending.

> "Allow the universe to guide you and the better your outcome will be"

Like many of the tarot trump cards, the Wheel of Fortune existed as a medieval allegory

The alchemical symbols for mercury, sulphur, solution/dissolution and salt are represented within the Wheel of Fortune, respectively illustrating the soul/spirit, physical human body and a human's journey through life

The Marseilles card shows the figures as three monkeys – symbols of folly

WHEEL of FORTUNE.

JUSTICE
TRUTH AND VIRTUE

An eye for an eye. You reap what you sow
with the Justice card

JUSTICE

NUMBER: 11

·

CARD

A crowned woman dressed in red
robes sits upon a stone throne
between two pillars. In her hands
are weighing scales and an
upright sword.

·

UPRIGHT

Truth, impartial judgement,
righted wrongs, karma, dealings
with the law, commitments and
contracts, law and order, balance
and equilibrium.

REVERSED

Avoiding responsibilities,
broken promises or contracts,
unfairness, abuse of power,
dishonesty, prejudice, corruption.

The cardinal virtue is symbolised by a monarchic figure sitting upon a throne of stone, a seat of power, between two pillars with a veil draped between them, just like the High Priestess. However, while the High Priestess' fruit-print veil conceals "the sea of unconscious" – indicated by the blue tone behind her – Justice's curtain hides the yellow glow of dawn, indicating a new day or new beginning. The dawn will only be revealed with wisdom and dignity.

Her position as the eighth card in the deck was swapped to the 11th in the Rider-Waite-Smith tarot so that the card corresponds to Libra, the astrological sign represented by scales. In Justice's left hand she holds a set of scales representing impartial judgement, truth and balance. Her crown, indicating her power and authority, bears a square to signify order and clarity. The square can also be seen on her breast, but this time with a circle within it. The image of a circle within a square is an important one within alchemy and is often shown within a larger triangle to represent the ultimate goal of alchemy: the philosopher's stone. The philosophical meaning of "squaring the circle", or capturing a circle within a square, means to see equally in all four directions, to treat all equally and justly. A circle is infinite, and symbolises the spiritual mind, while the square is physical, restraining and ordered.

In her right hand, she clasps a sword upright, a nod to medieval codes of chivalry, indicating she has sworn an oath to uphold virtue, and symbolising responsibility and power, but also mercy. The outcome could be favourable or unfavourable, but it will be fair. Justice is the law, and justice will be served according to physical facts, not feeling or spirit, and it will keep the balance. It will also likely be beyond your control.

> **"Justice's curtain hides the yellow glow of dawn, indicating a new day or new beginning. The dawn will only be revealed with wisdom and dignity"**

The balanced scales of justice: They must be equally weighted on either side so that the scales hang evenly

8 LA JUSTICE

Justice is one of the Platonic virtues seen across the tarot along with Strength, Temperance and Prudence (represented by the Hermit)

XI

The Justice card as depicted in a 15th century Visconti-Sforza tarot deck

JUSTICE .

XII

The symbol of the Hermetic Order of the Golden Dawn, of which Waite and Smith were members, shows the cross with the haloed sun beneath it, an image reflected in the Hanged Man trump card

THE HANGED MAN.

The Hanged Man from the Renault Tarot Of Besançon

LE PENDU

The 'Le Pendu' card from Oswald Wirth's 1889 tarot deck

THE HANGED MAN

SACRIFICE

A key figure in the soul's journey to enlightenment, with great sacrifice comes even greater insight

A ccording to Waite, the gallows from which the Hanged Man is tied to forms a 'tau cross' – a T-shape with the ends expanded in a similar manner to the Greek letter tau – "while the figure from the position of the legs forms a fylfot cross". The fylfot cross is a type of swastika that is associated with Anglo-Saxon culture. Before Hitler skewed our understanding of the swastika, these shapes were solar symbols, common across many ancient cultures across the globe.

While the card is commonly associated with martyrdom and specifically that of Christ, Waite's mention of a fylfot cross and the upside-down nature of the figure, along with the title itself – the Hanged Man – is more closely linked with Norse myth and, in particular, the tale of the god Odin, who hung himself upside down from a branch of Yggdrasil (the tree of life) in search for the higher wisdom and power harnessed by the Norns (the fates). The fable of Odin, and indeed the Hanged Man, teaches us that we must sacrifice our time, energy and even health on occasion to gain power, knowledge and to further our cause. It can be an arduous process, but in the end it will be worth the effort.

The Hanged Man is shown with the halo of Christ and an expression of deep entrancement, not suffering. The figure may be suspended, but he is not lifeless – Waite is keen to note this. He finds comfort in discomfort, and willingly perseveres through this ordeal, just as Odin willingly went through his, in order to achieve further power and knowledge. The cross and the halo around the figure's head can also be seen as mirroring the symbol of the Hermetic Order of the Golden Dawn – the sun of which is the halo around the Hanged Man's head.

This is a card of initiation. Waite also highlights the fact that the tree on which the figure is hung is alive, it lives on and flourishes despite the figure's ordeal. It expresses the relationship between the divine and the universe. As with The Fool, The Hanged Man's element is water, indicating fluidity and change rather than stagnation or fixed ideas.

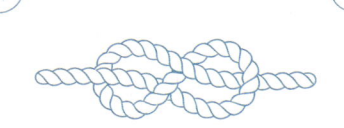

THE HANGED MAN

NUMBER: 12

CARD

A man with a halo, or nimbus, around his head hangs upside-down from a tree, his legs crossed, arms behind his back and look of contentment upon his face.

UPRIGHT

A reversal in attitude, perseverance, sacrifice, penance, spiritual growth, letting go.

REVERSED

Stagnation, needless sacrifice, delays, resistance, stalling, indecision, control. Don't be afraid to break free!

"It can be an arduous process, but in the end it will be worth the effort'

The Death trump card is associated with the astrological sign of Scorpio, which is fittingly linked to death and rebirth

The image of Death in the tarot is consistently represented by the skeletal figure of the Grim Reaper

Death's weapon of choice is the scythe, reminding us of the cyclical nature of sowing and reaping

DEATH
NEW BEGINNINGS

The great equaliser trumps all in the physical realm, but despite its negative connotations the 13th card is a card of significant positivity

The Death trump card consistently features the skeletal Grim Reaper figure. Developed during the late-medieval period, this image features in allegories known as the Dance Of Death – an artistic genre in which death triumphs over the living, no matter your age, sex or class, indicating the universality of death and its role as the great equaliser of all men.

In Hans Holbein's *The Dance Of Death* series of allegorical woodcuts, dating to the 16th century, the Grim Reaper is shown triumphing over a hermit, and the Death card trumps the Hermit. The Death card also shows the conclusion of the ritual of The Hanged Man, similarly, Holbein's series ends with the soul's transcendence of death – the ultimate goal of the Hanged Man. Death is always the 13th card, a number associated with bad luck, but also the trickster god, Loki, or biblically, the traitor, Judas. The Rider-Waite-Smith deck shows Death upon a pale white horse, referencing the Book Of Revelation's Four Horsemen of the Apocalypse. He wears black medieval plate armour – rather than the knight in shining armour, he is decked in darkness. Similarly to the medieval allegory, Death has slain a woman, a child, a king and a bishop – showing that no human, no matter how religious or powerful, can hide from death. However, Death holds a flag emblazoned with a white rose, a symbol of purity and innocence. For the Golden Dawn, this mystic rose symbolised rebirth.

In the background, there is a ship – a common symbol of the journey to the afterlife – sailing towards two towers, between which a sun is rising: the 'sun of immortality'. The two towers represent the twin pillars, an archetypal symbol of a passageway into the unknown – but the rising sun shows that this passageway is a new dawn and gateway into a positive place or a higher realm of enlightenment. Death is not the final card and therefore does not represent the end, rather it is a new beginning, one where the ego has been lost and the physical body has transcended and there is a new dawn of opportunity. The Death card represents the cyclic nature of all things – every ending is followed by a new beginning.

DEATH

NUMBER: 13

CARD
A skeletal knight rides a white horse and carries a black flag featuring a white rose. Upon the ground lay a king, a woman and a child, slain, while a bishop pleads to God for his life. In the distance, a ship sails towards a sunrise between two towers.

UPRIGHT
Transformational change, transcendence, progression, renewal, a blessing in disguise.

REVERSED
Resistance to change, lack of movement, loss, unwelcome or inevitable endings.

> **"Death is not the final card and therefore does not represent the end, rather it is a new beginning"**

TEMPERANCE
ACHIEVING HARMONY

Tempering and harmonising your states of being is essential to achieving the goal of the tarot: eternal life

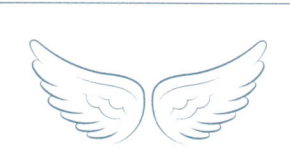

TEMPERANCE

NUMBER: 14

·

CARD
An angelic figure stands by a pool pouring fluid from one chalice to another while dipping one foot in the water.

·

UPRIGHT
Balance, peace, beauty, higher consciousness, moderation, harmony.

·

REVERSED
Imbalance, hastiness, excess, recklessness, avoidance and ignorance.

The final card in the second act of the Fool's Journey is curiously not Death but Temperance. Temperance is one of the cardinal virtues, dating back to classical times. She is almost always represented as a female who shows voluntary self-restraint and moderation. AE Waite, however, decided to represent Temperance as a genderless angel.

Temperance is shown pouring fluid between two chalices, commonly interpreted as watering down alcohol. Waite, however, suggests the liquid is that of the essences of life. Until the Renaissance, health and well-being were believed to be achieved by the harmony of the four humours: blood, phlegm, black bile and yellow bile. When one had a good temperament, they were believed to have a balance of these fluids.

One of Temperance's feet is in the water, the other is on the earth. According to Waite this illustrates the "nature of the essences". The water symbolises emotion, while the earth is grounding. Temperance has a solar disc upon their forehead and a triangle within a square on their chest, representing the seven-fold nature of man. Temperance is a reborn figure, free of ego and beside them in the background is a pathway leading to a peak on the verge of the horizon, where there hides a great light. This, says Waite, is "some part of the secret of eternal life". This light has a crown, whereas Temperance wears the sun.

Beside Temperance are flowers of purity: Iris, named for the Greek goddess of rainbows. She is a goddess of sea and sky and serves the gods their ambrosia. Temperance can also be compared to the Archangel Michael, sharing many of his traits. Temperance symbolises the Jungian concept of synchronicity: as above so below, inner and outer psyche, wet and dry.

> "One of Temperance's feet is in the water, the other is on the earth. Waite says this illustrates the 'nature of the essences'"

The Marseilles' Temperance exhibited angelic wings, a trait many subsequent decks have copied

TEMPERANCE

In Renaissance allegories Temperance was the cardinal virtue that defeated Wrath, in tarot she defeats Death

XIV

Temperance as envisioned by AE Waite and illustrated by Pamela Colman Smith

TEMPERANCE.

THE
DEVIL
TEMPTATION

A hero's quest is not complete without a final challenge. The Devil represents the greatest temptation yet – your own vices

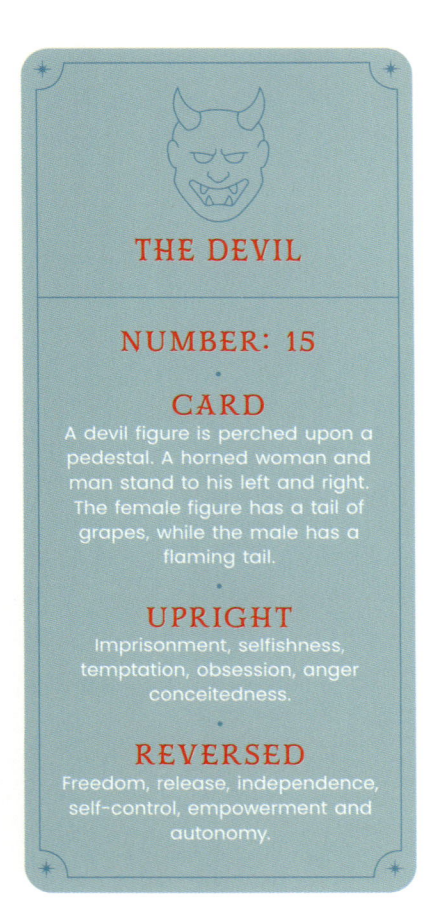

THE DEVIL

NUMBER: 15

CARD
A devil figure is perched upon a pedestal. A horned woman and man stand to his left and right. The female figure has a tail of grapes, while the male has a flaming tail.

UPRIGHT
Imprisonment, selfishness, temptation, obsession, anger conceitedness.

REVERSED
Freedom, release, independence, self-control, empowerment and autonomy.

The devil image featured on the Rider-Waite-Smith tarot is the horned goat of Mendes, also known as Baphomet, a symbol of balance in Western esoterica. It's based on an illustration by 19th century French occultist Éliphas Lévi, who wrote extensively about the meanings of the tarot, and features bird (or harpy) feet, goat horns, bat wings, a raised right hand and a lowered left. Lévi's figure represents occult science and magic.

In his left hand, he holds a torch, the symbol of passion, pointing down. His right hand shows the Jewish Kohanim hand signal – similar to the Sign of Benediction in Christianity and Catholicism, although often the fourth and little fingers are bent. This gesture mocks the Hierophant as it is traditionally the hand position a priest adopts while performing a blessing. Jewish mysticism, Kabbalah, had an influence on Western esotericism, particularly the Golden Dawn. The Devil's face is bestial, upon his forehead is a reversed pentacle, representing the triumph of matter over spirit, and he is perched upon a pedestal.

In front of the Devil are Adam and Eve. Their nudity has been perverted from innocence to sexual passion. Their tails nod to their respective trees in Eden – Eve's bears fruit as does the Tree Of Knowledge, while Adam's is ablaze to represent the Tree Of Life. They have fallen from grace and are chained to the pedestal, illustrating the fatality of material life. Waite notes that the bondsman above them is not to be their master forever, he is just doing his job.

The Devil trumps Temperance, as pleasure often tempts us to stray from moderation. Even Christ was tempted by the Devil in the desert, and on all heroic quests there must be a definitive final test. The Devil is the guardian of the higher realm, and indicates we are approaching our goal – it is the first card on the final stage of the Fool's Journey.

> **"The Devil is the guardian of the higher realm, and indicates we are approaching our goal"**

FORCE MAJEURE.

The Rider-Waite-Smith interpretation of The Devil trump card was heavily inspired by occultist Éliphas Lévi's Baphomet figure

Early hand-painted tarot decks curiously do not name the Devil card

The chaotic, illogical nature of the Devil is often represented through its mis-matched sex organs and animal traits

THE DEVIL .

The Rider-Waite-Smith Tower's roof is a crown being dismantled by lightning, representing destruction of the ego

There are many variations of the Tower card, including a crumbling stone structure and a tree hit by lightning

Both the Rider-Waite-Smith tarot and the Tarot of Piedmont Tower cards follow the model set by the Tarot of Marseilles

THE TOWER.

THE TOWER

DESTRUCTION

Destruction is necessary for recreation, and The Tower purges the soul with purifying fire, ready for you to emerge as your most evolved self yet!

In early tarot, the last seven cards illustrated the biblical book of Revelation – the story of the apocalypse, the Archangel Michael's victory over the armies of Satan, when the earth is cleansed by destruction. The dead are called up from their graves to face judgement and a new world is established where time stands still and death is abolished.

During the Renaissance, these ideas were mixed with other religious symbolism to express the journey of the soul into enlightenment. While the new world order is not lit by Christ in esotericism, it is indeed lit by a much higher state of consciousness that alchemists were keen to achieve. Many earlier tarot decks do not contain the Tower, some include an alternative card named Fire, Lightning, Thunderbolt, or even the House Of The Devil, however, the symbolism remains similar.

The Rider-Waite-Smith trump card follows the Marseilles deck, whereby a tower is struck by a lightning bolt, engulfing it in flames, which forces the roof to fly off. The Tower is the final destruction of the ego, burning away those selfish urges that prevent you from achieving enlightenment. Preconceived ideas are burnt away in order to ascend to the heavens or a higher state.

From above, a female and male figure fall. With a black background, to link the Tower to its predecessor, the Devil, these figures could be Adam and Eve, freed from their shackles. The flames descending with the couple appear to form the Hebrew letter yod, representing the number ten and a divine point of energy, which is used to form all other letters in the Hebrew alphabet.

The Tower is a sudden and significant shift, full of destruction and discomfort, but will result in something better.

> "The Tower is the destruction of the ego, burning away the selfish urges that prevent you from achieving enlightenment"

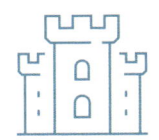

THE TOWER

NUMBER: 16

·

CARD

A tower is struck by lightning. Its top, a crown, has been lifted and fire descends. Two figures fall from the tower – one appears to have fallen while the other looks to have leapt.

·

UPRIGHT

Abrupt change, discomfort, transformation, upheaval, awakening.

REVERSED

Resisting change, delaying the inevitable, fear of letting go, control. Don't be afraid to break free!

The presence of the Star shining in the heavens represents the bright future that is ordained for those who draw this card

XVII

THE STAR.

The lady pouring out jugs on both water and land represents both the conscious and unconscious mind being nurtured

Some images show a king bearing a gift under a star – drawing from the tale of the wise men heading for the new start promised by the nativity

THE
STAR
NEW HOPES

This card reminds us to keep a positive outlook and trust that the universe will provide the things we need

The stars blaze strongly in the blackness of the night sky and this card represents their conquest of the darkness. The Star card is one of the most positive in the entire tarot deck. Drawing this card means that the heavens are truly shining on you. On the card itself is not just a star, however. It shows a woman pouring out liquid which represents the nourishing forces that are at work in the world. One stream of water falls on the earth and one into a pool. Both the subconscious and the conscious mind are working together and being renewed.

When the Star is drawn in the upright position it is a supportive sign. Things are about to go very well indeed – as long as you trust in the forces around you. This should bring about a sense of hope or inspire you to be hopeful. Take that feeling and make it work for you. Try new things and have faith that they will turn out for the best. This card can also be about inspiration and instinct. It may be pointing to a need for fresh ideas, safe in the knowledge that they will be the right ones.

When this card is reversed it usually means that you have lost hope and no longer trust that the universe will provide. Are you worried that nothing will ever come your way? Perhaps you began a new endeavour with great plans but are finding them frustrated. You fear that you will never reach your goal. The reversed Star is a warning not to give up. You were right in your initial feelings. Trust yourself.

The Star is a manifestation of the connection between the individual and the universe. People can feel alone and disconnected. Just as the star casts its light onto the Earth from a huge distance this card reminds us that we are part of a greater whole. Understanding that helps renew our hopes that we are not as alone as we fear.

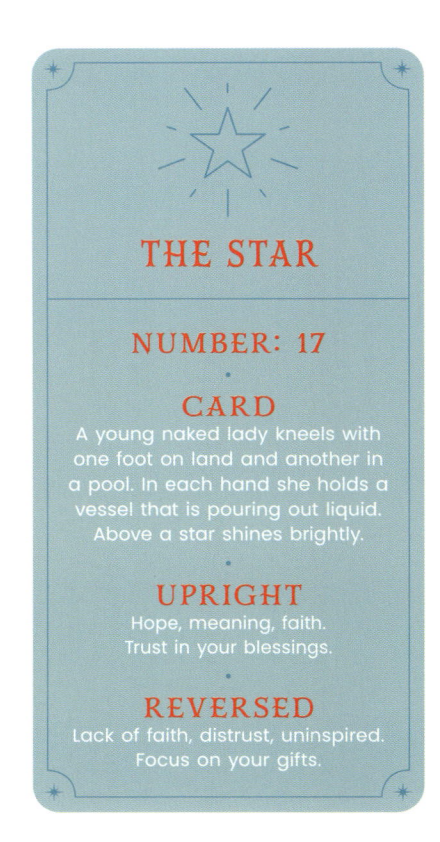

THE STAR

NUMBER: 17

CARD
A young naked lady kneels with one foot on land and another in a pool. In each hand she holds a vessel that is pouring out liquid. Above a star shines brightly.

UPRIGHT
Hope, meaning, faith. Trust in your blessings.

REVERSED
Lack of faith, distrust, uninspired. Focus on your gifts.

> **"The Star is a manifestation of the connection between the individual and the universe"**

THE
MOON
FEARS AND ILLUSIONS

The Moon is a card of fear and doubt but also one which can point the way to releasing yourself from their snare

THE MOON

NUMBER: 18
·
CARD
Under the light of
a full moon's face a dog
and a wolf sit howling.
A crayfish crawls out from
a pool of water.

UPRIGHT
Illusion, anxiety, fear.
Listen to your doubts.

REVERSED
Repressed emotions, confusion,
self-delusion. Let go of your fears!

The appearance of the Moon in tarot can be scary. The dog and wolf shown howling at the serene face of the moon represent the fears inside all of us – even when we have nothing to be afraid of. The crayfish which emerges from a hidden pool is like the thoughts which can be lurking deep in our subconscious which hold us back.

When the Moon is drawn in the upright position it can be a real warning about things going on, which you are not even fully aware of. If you are having doubts about a situation you should heed your feelings. Now is not the time to act. Caution is needed because your subconscious may have realised things that have not yet percolated into your waking mind. Watch out for those who may be acting against your best interests.

The unstable nature of the moon is also represented here. Although the moon is always the same, it seems to wax and wane, sometimes bright and sometimes dark. Are you being hoodwinked by someone? Illusions are not always easy to spot.

When the Moon is reversed, it is the time to take actions that you have been afraid to try. Doubts and fears can be useful when they guard us from danger, but can be a trap that holds us back if we listen to every anxiety. Examine each of your fears closely and see whether you are being led astray by them. Cast them off and realise you are free. Just as dogs bark at the harmless moon, you are being tricked by your instincts.

Initially, the Moon card can seem almost wholly negative in its warnings and revelations of our mental weaknesses, but it is a useful sign that things can change. The moon goes from new to full and back again without harm and we must be open to making changes too.

> "Examine each of your fears closely and
> see whether you are being led astray
> by them"

The dog and wolf, which howl at the full moon, represent the fears that fill our mind and threaten at times to overwhelm us

Some variations of the Moon card show wise people closely studying its face to interpret its constant changes of appearance

The Moon has long been tied to the passage of time and the thread of fate – which is sometimes shown in the hand of a lady looking at the moon

XVIII

THE MOON.

THE
SUN
REVELATION AND RENEWAL

No card has as positive a reading as the Sun – so long as you understand what it is really telling you

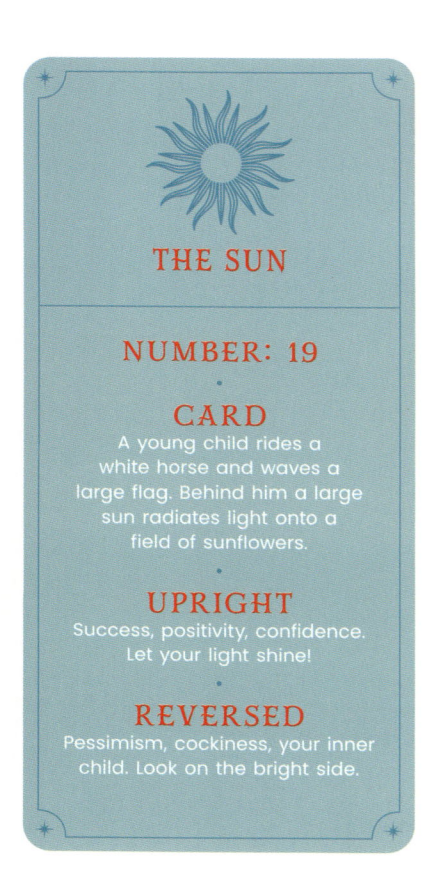

THE SUN

NUMBER: 19

CARD
A young child rides a white horse and waves a large flag. Behind him a large sun radiates light onto a field of sunflowers.

UPRIGHT
Success, positivity, confidence. Let your light shine!

REVERSED
Pessimism, cockiness, your inner child. Look on the bright side.

Many view this as a tarot card that has no negative meaning – whichever way you look at it, the sun is still dazzlingly bright! The warmth of the sun radiates out from this card. However, the sun is not the only thing depicted on this card. Below the sun there is a young child, naked and in a state of innocence, basking in its glow. It rides a placid white horse, another symbol of innocence and power, while holding a large banner aloft. This represents the inborn power and confidence that we can all tap into.

When the Sun is drawn in its upright position, you should be filled with your own inner light. This is a card of abundance. There is enough energy both within and without for you to do and dare anything. You should also be willing to share your joy and power with others. There is plenty to share. Be like the sun and warm those around you.

This card can be a good predictor in all areas of your life. When it refers to health, it can be read as a return to vitality and well-being. If the card is drawn in a position of relationships, it can mean passion, love, and truth. If you are wondering whether a move in business or work is the right one, then the Sun can be your guiding light to success.

When the Sun is reversed, some interpretations can be less positive, but never fully negative. It always serves to remind us that there is a spiritual support that will never fail. In the reversed position, it may be that you have lost your zest for life and you should try to recapture it. The obstacles that you are facing will be temporary, so long as you keep your positivity.

Don't ever go so far that you become cocky, however. An innocent willingness to succeed is the key. This card tells us to embrace our inner child and always be open to new things. After all, the sun always rises.

> **"It always serves to remind us that there is a spiritual support that will never fail"**

The huge figure of the Sun blazes out from this card and represents the powers of positivity and warmth

In this image from an early tarot deck, a child grasps the sun, just as the card encourages us to grab hold of opportunities

Some tarot decks show two children together – they are united and protected by the sun in a state of innocence

THE SUN .

This card shows people called by the messenger of God from their graves for judgement at Doomsday

XX

JUDGEMENT.

Those who are called to judgement are shown naked, because before God, all pretence and disguise is stripped away and nothing is hidden

20 LE JUGEMENT

The trumpets which the angel uses represent the call to judgement – just as this card calls on questioners to make a choice

JUDGEMENT

THE CARD OF CHOICES

This card serves to remind us that our choices shape our lives – and warns us to choose carefully

In the New Testament St Paul, in his first letter to the Corinthians, describes how the dead will be raised and resurrected at the end of days. This scene is shown on the Judgement card, with those who were once dead now called forth from their tombs for divine judgement. The message is clear – not even death can shield us from judgement. The message of this card is the same. Whether we like it or not, we all face judgement in our lives and must make judgements ourselves.

The broader meaning of this card encompasses awakenings and new beginnings. No matter what the situation is, and they don't come much grimmer than death, there is always the chance to start afresh. Though judgement can be unpleasant process, a person must open themselves up to the risk of pain if they want to embrace opportunities. In predictions, Judgement can have a straightforward message – you may face a legal case, an evaluation at work, or a tricky moral dilemma. It can also point you towards the need to embody your best self, so that you may judge others fairly. You must resurrect the best version of yourself. In the upright position this card can also mean that you are being judged too harshly by others.

In the reversed position, Judgement is a call for reflection. It can represent a person having too much self-doubt or holding on to blame. A bad judgement has been made that is still causing trouble. It may also mean that a person is refusing to make a choice. Without making a final judgement, a matter will never be resolved. If you are taking part in a legal action and have drawn this card it may not go well for you.

This card can have troubling implications but it is a call to action. We must strip ourselves of those things that are holding us back, if we are to be released for a new chance.

JUDGEMENT

NUMBER: 20

CARD
An angel in the sky blasts a trumpet and naked people rise from their graves to answer the call to judgement.

UPRIGHT
Judgement, new awakenings, rebirth. Don't be afraid to start again!

REVERSED
Doubt, ignoring a chance, failure to learn from the past. Grab hold of opportunities!

> "The broader meaning of this card encompasses awakenings and new beginnings"

The woman steps towards the future while also looking back to the past – the two cannot be separated

In some tarot decks, the world supports the human figure

The lion, the bull, the angel, and the man are symbolic representations of the classical elements and signs of the zodiac

THE WORLD.

THE
WORLD
VOYAGE AND SUCCESS

This card is a sign of wholeness and completion and suggests your life coming to fruition

The World card is the summation of the Major Arcana. It is the end of the cycle and also the beginning of the next one. As the world passes through its seasons without end, so do the cycles of our lives. The card shows a human seemingly dancing above the Earth. They move forwards but also look backwards. A circle does not have a beginning or an end and time must be viewed as a whole too.

When the World is drawn in the upright position it points towards completion. This can be spiritual, which means that you have become unified in your mind and spirit. It can also mean that a goal you have been pursuing has come to its ultimate completion. If you have not yet achieved your aims, then this card is telling you that now you are in the best position to do it. All of the troubles and problems that you have overcome have led you to this point – you are ready for this.

If the World card is in the reversed position, it could mean that there has been a slowing recently in your path towards wholeness and completion. Have you started to question yourself unnecessarily? It may be an indication that you have come close to reaching your goals, but you have taken your eye off the ball. You need to re-focus and put everything into your efforts.

When the World is reversed, it could also be a warning to you that there will be an unexpected delay. However, you should not let this derail you, because whatever caused it can also be overcome. Even when it is drawn upside down, the World is not a negative card.

This card is one of the best possible signals from the tarot. You may find that whatever happens turns out for the best. Even mistakes will turn themselves, in the end, to your benefit.

THE WORLD

NUMBER: 21

CARD
A naked lady dances within a wreath. She is watched by a man, an eagle, a lion, and a bull.

UPRIGHT
Accomplishment, travel, completion. You have reached your goal.

REVERSED
Seeking closure, delays, frustration. Hold on, you'll get there!

"Even when it is drawn upside down, the World is not a negative card"

THE MINOR ARCANA

The cards of the Minor Arcana form the bulk of the tarot deck, and are central to guiding querents through their journey to understanding

The 56 cards that make up the Minor Arcana are the foundation of any tarot deck and form the vast bulk of its contents. Whilst an understanding of the cards of the Major Arcana is vital to any reader, the nuances of the Minor Arcana cannot be overlooked if one is to work with the cards to their full potential.

Just like a deck of playing cards, a tarot deck has four suits. However, whilst playing cards are instantly recognisable as the hearts, diamonds, clubs and spades, the suits of tarot can vary depending on the deck and the geographical territory from which it originated. Today, most readers recognise the suits that were used in the immensely popular Rider-Waite deck, those of Pentacles, Wands, Swords and Cups. Other popular decks do make substitutions though, so in the influential Tarot of Marseilles readers will find not Pentacles but Coins, and Clubs in the place of Wands. Likewise, when Aleister Crowley designed his esoteric Book of Thoth, he replaced Pentacles with Disks. Despite the nomenclature though, the elemental significance and meanings of the suits are, as a rule, retained.

The Minor Arcana are, essentially, the minutiae of life. They reflect our daily journey, whether it is remarkable or more mundane, and they are able to uniquely reflect even the most seemingly insignificant day-to-day situations that may be having an impact on us. Perhaps most significantly, the cards of the Minor Arcana can signify a more transitory situation than those reflected by the Major Arcana. Whilst they do not necessarily speak of matters that may seem enormously significant though, every stitch in the tapestry of life has an impact on the overall pattern. By listening to and interpreting the messages communicated by the Minor Arcana during a reading, a querant might be able to make even a small change to a minor situation and change the wider picture to a degree that might seem surprising.

Despite its name, there is nothing minor about the Minor Arcana when it comes to its place in the tarot deck. Without a thorough understanding of these cards and what the suits themselves stand for, a wealth of significance and nuance will be lost from any tarot reading. Read in concert with the Major Arcana, they are important building blocks in the process of understanding the tarot.

Every stitch in the tapestry of life has an impact on the overall pattern

> "The cards of the Minor Arcana can signify a more transitory situation than those reflected by Major Arcana"

The cards of the Minor Arcana are the fundamental building blocks of any tarot pack and cannot be ignored

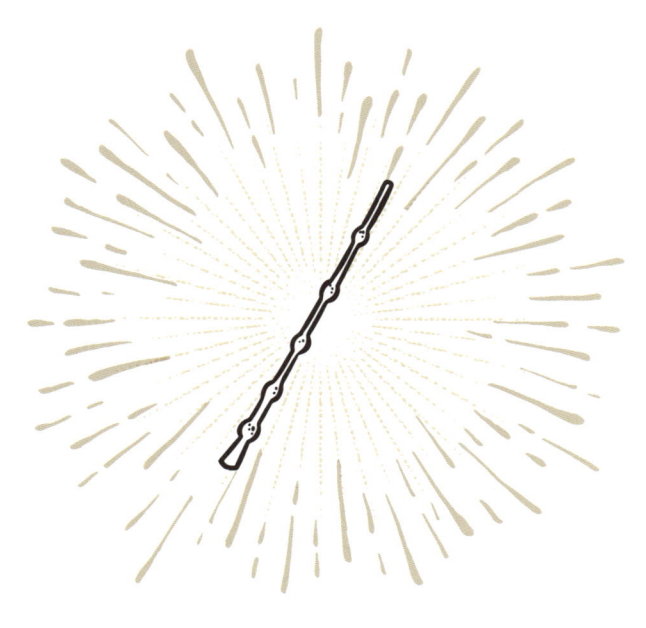

THE SUIT OF WANDS

If things are feeling fruitful and rich with creativity, the suit of Wands might make an appearance

The suit of Wands is associated with the element of fire. And just like fire, the Wands are filled with heat and energy, but they can be volatile and difficult to handle. However, the suit of Wands brings with it many positive qualities. It is a suit that promises inspiration and the drive and willpower to see through any project, no matter what it might be. It is associated with creativity and change, and the ability to make positive changes happen.

If Wands appear in a reading, the querent can look forward to some passionate, if sometimes temperamental times. Just as fire can warm or burn us though, so too can the suit of Wands prove to be anything but positive. As a temperamental suit, when Wands are reversed they can bring with them dangers of their own. If the fire that flares within the Wands is allowed to get out of control, it can leave a person badly burned. However, even the most raging fire can eventually be controlled, and so too can the power of Wands be quelled and harnessed, to once again bring light and heat to any situation.

> "The querent can look forward to passionate, if sometimes temperamental times"

ACE OF
WANDS

CARD

A hand emerges from a cloud in a clear sky, clutching a wand of wood on which leaves are growing, whilst leaves scatter the air around the bough too. On the ground below, the trees are green and the grass looks healthy, and a calm river winds lazily into the distance, towards low mountains on the horizon. A white castle stands atop a verdant hill, looking out over the river.

•

UPRIGHT

Excitement, potential, creativity

•

REVERSED

Lack of creativity, chances lost, promises abandoned

TWO OF
WANDS

CARD

A man stands looking out over a body of water, holding a wand in one hand and contemplating a globe in the other. A second wand is attached to the low crenellated wall in front of him, beyond which is a cheery green landscape and a calm expanse of water. If the man wishes to travel onward to adventure and new horizons, it looks as though his journey will be a tranquil one.

•

UPRIGHT

Planning, travel, decision-making

•

REVERSED

Failure to plan, avoiding change, indecision

THREE OF
WANDS

CARD

A man in a bright cape stands with his back to the viewer, looking out over the sun-drenched calm waters beneath. He stands on solid ground, holding one wand while two others are standing in the ground around him, each with new green leaves. Beneath the sunlit golden sky, three boats cross the water on their way to unknown destinations, or perhaps the distant shore that the man is contemplating one day seeing.

UPRIGHT

Travel, freedom, growth

•

REVERSED

Clinging to the past, frustrations, obstacles

FOUR OF
WANDS

CARD

A man and woman wearing classical robes and laurel crowns celebrate beneath an arch made of four wands. They are decorated with an archway of rich green foliage, flowers, fruit and ribbons, and new shoots sprout from the boughs. The couple hold flowing bouquets and behind them, more figures dance together, celebrating the couple before the walls of a castle and beneath a golden sky.

UPRIGHT

Celebration, family, community

•

REVERSED

Family discord, lack of teamwork, self-doubt

FIVE OF
WANDS

CARD

Though the sky is cloudless and the ground is verdant with growth, the five young men depicted on this card don't see that. Instead, they're too intent on fighting, using their wands as weapons despite the new shoots that are sprouting from them. Nobody appears willing to back down, and with the men apparently evenly matched, it remains to be seen whether there can truly be any victors.

UPRIGHT

Conflict, anger, rivalry

•

REVERSED

Resolution, peace, solutions

SIX OF
WANDS

CARD

A man rides a white horse at what appears to be a stately pace, both of them dressed in flowing capes. He wears a laurel crown and carries a wand, upon which another laurel crown is mounted. A cheerful crowd have gathered to greet the man, who is apparently a returning hero, and they too carry wands. They flourish them skywards in a celebration of the man's return and his achievements.

UPRIGHT

Victory, praise, acclaim

•

REVERSED

Arrogance, disappointment, disgrace

SEVEN OF
WANDS

CARD

A young man wields a wand against six others that appear to assail him from below. He stands beneath a clear blue sky, upon the green grass, astride a narrow, calm trickle of water, but whilst one of his feet is on solid ground, the other is dangerously close to what looks like a cliff edge. His expression is determined, his stance strong and undaunted, but his unmatching shoes suggest that he isn't on solid ground just yet.

·

UPRIGHT

Stamina, perseverance, self-assertiveness

·

REVERSED

Weakness, burnout, surrender

EIGHT OF
WANDS

CARD

Eight wands fly through the air, heading towards the earth from left to right. Who threw them is a mystery, but each is sprouting fresh leaves and they appear strong and healthy. Beneath the staves, the grass is green and in the distance, a small white building stands atop a hill, surrounded by healthy trees. Soon the wands will land and perhaps their leaves will take root.

·

UPRIGHT

Speed, progression, striking out

·

REVERSED

Bad timing, chances missed, slowness

NINE OF
WANDS

CARD

A man stands alone, clutching a single wand protectively. His sleeves are rolled up and his head is bandaged, whilst his expression is watchful and determined. Behind him, eight further leafy wands rise up towards the sky, apparently blocking his only escape route. He stands upon featureless stone, but behind the staves, the earth is green and bright. The sky is clear and in the distance, all we can see is more settled countryside.

·

UPRIGHT

Persistence, resilience, making a stand

·

REVERSED

Exhaustion, stalemate, stubborn

TEN OF
WANDS

CARD

A man trudges onwards, his back bent and his arms wrapped around the bundle of wands that he is trying to carry. The man's head is bowed towards the wands as he leans into the weight of his burden, blocking his vision of what is up ahead. On the horizon are green trees and a castle, where he will soon be able to lay down his burden and survey the fruits of his labours.

·

UPRIGHT

Overburdened, struggle, responsibility

·

REVERSED

Stress, burnout, lack of delegation

PAGE OF
WANDS

CARD

A young man stands alone in a barren desert, dressed in richly coloured clothes, patterned with a lizard and a cheery hat with a feather. His head is held high and he looks out towards the future, both hands holding a tall, sturdy wand that will offer him support on his journey. The young man appears determined and ready for adventure in more productive lands than the desert where he currently finds himself.

UPRIGHT

Happiness, excitement, optimism

•

REVERSED

Dull, indecisive, directionless

KNIGHT OF
WANDS

CARD

A knight in armour and a tabard decorated with lizards rides upon a rearing, sturdy horse. The knight's visor is open and a brightly-coloured plume flutters above it. One hand holds the patterned reins, the other a wand. Both man and horse wear determined expressions as they look ahead, but there is perhaps the slightest hint of doubt in the young man's eyes, despite his armour.

UPRIGHT

Adventure, fearlessness, confidence

·

REVERSED

Anger, recklessness, arrogance

QUEEN OF
WANDS

CARD

A woman dressed in golden robes sits atop a richly-appointed throne. She wears a cape and a crown and holds in one hand a tall wand, whilst in the other she holds a sunflower. The throne is also decorated with sunflowers and painted effigies of rampant lions, images of fertile life and strength. At her feet a black cat sits, looking out of the card with inquisitive green eyes that suggest the woman's intuition and instinct.

UPRIGHT

Joy, courage, confidence

•

REVERSED

Overbearing, selfish, envious

KING OF
WANDS

CARD

The king sits on his throne wearing opulent orange robes and a cape decorated with lizards. He wears a golden crown and a necklace featuring a lion's head, while he holds a wand in one hand. The throne itself is golden, decorated with more lizards and lions, and he appears to be self-possessed, calm and confident. On the stone plinth of the throne, a small lizard waits, looking out in the same direction as the king.

UPRIGHT

Loyalty, leadership, meeting challenges

•

REVERSED

Impulsive, bullying, bitterness

THE — SUIT OF CUPS

Emotion, creativity and intuition of all kinds find their expression in the suit of Cups

The suit of Cups is associated strongly with intuition and emotion, and often signifies relationships. It is a suit of empathy and artistic expression, offering great promise if one is willing to go with feeling over facts now and then.

The suit of Cups is the suit of water, which flows through many of the cards in one form or another. Just as fire can warm or burn, water can nurture and nourish but it can also be dangerous, so things in the suit of Cups aren't always tranquil. When it presents in a less positive sense, this suit can represent an unwillingness to take a logical approach even when that is necessary, or can warn that we are becoming so absorbed in our daydreams and fantasies that we are losing sight of the real world and what we need to achieve. When that happens, creative blocks can follow.

When the suit of Cups is predominant in a reading, it is a distinct sign that a little intuition might go a long way. Sometimes, following one's hunch can pay rich dividends in sometimes unexpected aspects of life.

> **"The suit of Cups is the suit of water, which flows through many of the cards"**

ACE OF
CUPS

CARD

A hand emerges from the clouds with its palm open. Resting on the palm is a golden cup, from which water overflows, running down into the calm waters below, where lily pads float. Above the cup is a dove, completing the peaceful scene. The open palm appears to be inviting us to take a drink from the cup and its crystal, abundant water, and experience the promise that it brings.

UPRIGHT

Creativity, inspiration, love

REVERSED

Unloved, creative blocks, loss

TWO OF
CUPS

CARD

Dressed in bright robes and floral crowns, a man and a woman are exchanging cups before a background of blooming trees and a cosy cottage. Above them is a chimera, watchful and protective. The couple on the card has clearly reached a place of understanding, whether romantically or platonically, and each knows that they can trust the other as they move ahead with the partnership they have forged.

UPRIGHT

Partnership, companionship, connection

REVERSED

Division, rejection, solitude

THREE OF
CUPS

CARD

Three women are celebrating together, dancing in a circle with their cups raised in celebration. They wear colourful, loose robes and floral wreaths in their loose hair, while they are surrounded by an abundance of fruit and produce. The women are enjoying all that they have but, rather than celebrating alone, are sharing their joy with one another. Though we cannot see the face of one woman, the smiles of her friends suggest there is only warmth between the trio.

UPRIGHT

Celebration, friendship, community

·

REVERSED

Loneliness, reclusiveness, over-indulgence

FOUR OF
CUPS

CARD

A young man sits cross-legged beneath a tree, his arms folded across his chest as he contemplates three cups that stand before him. Despite what he has, his expression is gloomy and he appears discontented with a lot. In fact, the man is so focused on what he has that he cannot see the hand emerging from the clouds to offer him another cup, and the opportunity to add to the things he already has.

UPRIGHT

Contemplation, apathy, gloom

·

REVERSED

Self-awareness, sadness, accepting what cannot change

FIVE OF
CUPS

CARD

A figure cloaked in black stands on the shore of a river, its head bowed in what appears to be sadness. On the ground around him are five cups, two of which are standing up, whilst three have fallen over and spilt their contents upon the ground. Beyond the seemingly impassable river is a castle, but the man cannot see how to reach it. If he lifts his head though, he will discover a bridge up ahead.

UPRIGHT

Grief, sadness, loss

•

REVERSED

Moving on, turning the corner, finding acceptance

SIX OF
CUPS

CARD

A little boy and girl play in a beautiful garden, surrounded by cups filled with flowers and with a cosy-looking home behind them. The boy is handing his friend one of the cups and is taking time to inhale the scene of flowers that it contains. The children are safe and protected, with few cares, and seem to offer us an idyllic image of childhood and a sentimental sense of nostalgia.

UPRIGHT

Comfort, nostalgia, tradition

•

REVERSED

Leaving home, getting stuck, focusing too much on the past

SEVEN OF
CUPS

CARD

A figure stands with their back to the querent, reacting in wonder at the seven cups that have appeared in the clouds before them. Each cup contains a different offering, from castles to jewels, snakes and dragons, and it isn't clear which the figure should choose for the best outcome. In fact, the person can't even be sure that the cups and their contents are real, or daydreams that may disappear.

·

UPRIGHT

Indecisiveness, daydreams, making choices

·

REVERSED

Too many options, confusion, distraction

EIGHT OF
CUPS

CARD

A man turns his back on eight cups and walks away, crossing the river as he heads towards the distant mountains. The moon looks down at him, but provides little light to illuminate his path. Though he cannot know what awaits him in the mountains, the man knows that it is time to leave behind all that he has and seek a new challenge, wherever it may take him.

·

UPRIGHT

Letting go, abandonment, searching

·

REVERSED

Feeling stuck, avoidance, avoiding change

NINE OF
CUPS

CARD

A merry man sits on a stool with his arms folded and a look of contentment on his face. Behind him stands an ornate shelf, on which nine cups are displayed, and he is clearly very happy with all that he has managed to achieve. The man wears a vibrant red headdress, perhaps signifying that he has achieved all that he has by using his mind.

•

UPRIGHT

Achievement, contentment, attainment

•

REVERSED

Disappointment, feeling unfulfilled, haughtiness

TEN OF
CUPS

CARD

A rainbow blazes in the sky, containing ten cups. Beneath it, a man and woman embrace as they herald the rainbow's appearance, their arms raised in celebration, and a little boy and girl dance happily together. Their home is cosy, the river that runs through their nourished land is calm and clear, and it appears they have all they could wish for. There is no doubt that this family is a happy and fortunate one.

•

UPRIGHT

Harmony, domesticity, happiness

•

REVERSED

Family feuds, trouble at home, separation

PAGE OF
CUPS

CARD

A young man, wearing a bright tunic and clothes, holds a cup from which a fish emerges. Though the man looks happy and perhaps a little dreamy, the waves behind him are choppy. The blue hat and tunic the young man wears suggest that perhaps his head is in the clouds, and until he deals with the fish in his cup, he can't use the vessel for anything else.

UPRIGHT

Being a dreamer, naivety, innocence

•

REVERSED

Immaturity, insecurity, disappointments

KNIGHT OF
CUPS

CARD

Dressed in armour decorated with fish and with wings upon his helmet, the knight looks self-assured and calm on his white steed. Although he isn't charging into battle, he is offering the cup he holds proudly, as though making a gesture of peace or friendship. This knight has no need to fight at the moment, but is instead a picture of serenity and calm despite, or perhaps because of, his armour.

UPRIGHT

Artistry, negotiation, diplomacy

•

REVERSED

Bad moods, disappointment, lack of tact

QUEEN OF
CUPS

CARD

A woman sits upon a throne decorated with cherubs, her attention focused on the ornate cup that she holds. Her throne is positioned on the seashore, and her feet are almost, but not quite, resting in the surf at the edge of the land. The woman contemplates the cup, the handles of which are in the shape of angels, and appears utterly at peace with herself and her surroundings.

UPRIGHT

Kindness, care, compassion

•

REVERSED

Neediness, fragility, insecurity

KING OF
CUPS

CARD

A man sits on a throne that seems to float on the very surface of the water itself. He wears an ornate crown and a necklace shaped like a fish, and his expression is calm and thoughtful. A fish leaps from the water to one side of the man, whilst to the other side is a boat, its sails unfurled. These two elements represent the balance between the real world and the world of emotion.

UPRIGHT

Wisdom, balance, calm

·

REVERSED

Manipulation, worry, stress

THE
SUIT OF
SWORDS

When it comes to decisive action and powerful communication, the Swords are a significant suit

The suit of Swords is a suit of logic and rational thought, associated with the element of air. Just like a sharp-bladed sword, the Swords are straight to the point and sometimes sharp. The strength of Swords lies in its focus on thought, communication and logic. Rather than emotion, the suit of Swords finds its focus in clarity and knowledge. Swords offer the opportunity for power and courage, but they can also be the source of conflict, and like all suits of the tarot, Swords can have their weaknesses too. Just as the weapon from which it takes its name can do harm, so too can the Swords of the tarot be reflective of the power to do harm and cause distress.

Whenever a tarot reading is predominantly swords, it is likely that the querent is struggling with mental conflict and possible difficult decisions. Swords can cause harm or cause help, but they can also protect, and anyone who sees a reading that is filled with Swords would do well to keep an eye on events that are happening around them, and may have an impact on their own lives.

> **"Rather than emotion, the suit of Swords finds its focus in clarity and knowledge"**

ACE OF
SWORDS

CARD

A hand reaches from a cloud, gripping the hilt of a sharp, silver sword. At the tip of the blade is a crown, draped with holly on one side and seaweed on the other, while flecks of gold are scattered around the hilt. On the earth below the hand are mountains, but the vast majority of the image is occupied by a sky that is clear, other than the cloud from which the sword is emerging.

·

UPRIGHT

New projects, breakthrough, clarity

·

REVERSED

Confusion, loss of focus, chaos

TWO OF
SWORDS

CARD

A woman dressed in a simple, white robe sits on a bench before a body of water. The woman is blindfolded and her arms are crossed over her chest. In each hand she holds a sword so long that the tips of the blades are outside the frame of the image. A crescent moon shines down over the water, and though rocks rise out of the waves, behind her is a distant island.

·

UPRIGHT

Split loyalties, denial, difficult choices

·

REVERSED

Confusion, no good choice, indecision

THREE OF
SWORDS

CARD

A large, red heart occupies the centre of the card. It has been pierced with three crossed sword blades, one straight down through the middle, one that enters through the top-left, and one that pierces the heart through the top-right. Dark storm clouds have gathered above the heart, and heavy rain lashes down. There is no sign of solid ground or the earth below the storm.

UPRIGHT

Heartbreak, sorrow, disillusion

·

REVERSED

Optimism, forgiveness, moving on

FOUR OF
SWORDS

CARD

The stone effigy of a knight rests atop his tomb, serene and undisturbed. Above the tomb is a stained-glass window, not all of which is visible, showing a mother and child in a colourful scene. Directly over the upper torso and head of the effigy is a plaque on which three swords hang, their blades pointed towards his body. A fourth sword is carved in the stone side of the tomb, beneath the effigy's back.

UPRIGHT

Deep thought, rest, recuperation

•

REVERSED

Exhaustion, breakdown, stress

FIVE OF
SWORDS

CARD

A young man watches two other men walk away. While their heads are bowed in defeat, he appears smug and self-satisfied. In one hand he holds two swords, their points upright. In the other hand he holds a third, its blade pointing at the earth. Two discarded swords are on the ground. The sky above is cloudy, and over the water behind the three men, distant islands can be seen.

UPRIGHT

Ambitious, dishonesty, ruthlessness

•

REVERSED

Resolution, compromise, reconciliation

SIX OF
SWORDS

CARD

Three people, two adults and a child, are on a small boat heading away. Stabbed into the bottom of the boat are six swords. One of the two seated figures is huddled into a blanket, and though the huddled figure looks unhappy, she is finally heading for pastures new thanks to the man who steers the boat out into calm waters. On a distant island on the horizon, blossoming trees promise a peaceful haven.

UPRIGHT

Positive change, moving on, travel

•

REVERSED

Resistance to positive change, feeling stuck in a rut, instability

SEVEN OF
SWORDS

CARD

A smug-looking man runs away from a trio of brightly patterned tents, carrying five swords. Two further swords are embedded in the ground behind him. Though the sky overhead is bright and three other figures are gathered together in silhouette behind him, this man is fleeing with the swords that he appears to have stolen. What he doesn't realise is that the silhouetted men appear to have spotted him trying to get away with his crime.

·

UPRIGHT

Lies, deception, cheating

·

REVERSED

Confession, remorse, conscience

EIGHT OF
SWORDS

CARD

A blindfolded woman in an orange gown stands with her hands bound behind her back, her body encircled by bonds and her head bowed. Behind her are eight swords that are embedded in the earth to cage her, but nothing stands before her. The ground beneath her feet is waterlogged, and dark clouds streak the sky overhead. On the horizon is a rocky outcrop, upon which the towers of a castle can be seen.

·

UPRIGHT

Restrictions, victimisation, anxiety

·

REVERSED

Freedom, perspective, taking control

NINE OF
SWORDS

CARD

A figure sits up in bed, their face hidden in their hands as though in despair. Though the bed covers are bright and patterned, the room behind them is in pitch darkness, and nine swords split the blackness. The bed is decorated with an image of two people fighting, and it seems as if the figure in the bed is beset by upsetting images both in their nightmares and in their environment.

·

UPRIGHT

Anxiety, trauma, stress

·

REVERSED

Seeking help, recovery, hope

TEN OF
SWORDS

CARD

A man lies on the ground, covered by a red cloth, with ten swords stabbed into his body, though there are no wounds or blood. Above him, the sky is pitch dark and beneath him the earth is barren. However, behind the body of the man is a wide expanse of calm water and on the far side of the water is a mountainous landscape. Above the mountains the sky is bright and clear, suggesting a new dawn

·

UPRIGHT

Betrayal, exhaustion, defeat

·

REVERSED

Turning a corner, learning lessons, the only way is up

PAGE OF
SWORDS

CARD

A young woman stands atop a hill, poised for action and gripping a sword, as though she is about to swing it. She looks ready for anything and defiant, but while the ground beneath her feet is green, behind her clouds are gathering heavy winds that whip distant trees. Far above her head, a flock of birds flies above the clouds, untroubled by the gale that whips up the woman's hair.

UPRIGHT

Planning, curiosity, patience

•

REVERSED

Cynicism, bluntness, manipulation

KNIGHT OF
SWORDS

CARD

A knight in shining armour atop a white steed charges into battle, his sword raised and his mouth open as though to give a war cry. He is moving fast, carried by his horse, and they are leaping from one side of the card to the other. Storm clouds crowd the blue sky and the trees are blown by heavy winds, but he is charging against them.

UPRIGHT

Opportunity, impulsivity, going for it

•

REVERSED

Opportunity missed, lack of focus, directionless

QUEEN OF
SWORDS

CARD

A poised woman sits in a throne, and is dressed in a white robe, a cape of blue decorated with clouds and a crown of golden butterflies. She holds one hand aloft, her palm open. In her other hand is a sword, suggesting an image of justice and judgment. The woman's clear, intelligent expression tells us that she is not a dreamer, and will not be easily fooled.

UPRIGHT

Perceptive, independent, open-minded

·

REVERSED

Criticism, cruelty, bitterness

KING OF
SWORDS

CARD

A man sits on a throne, dressed in a white and orange robe and purple cape, a golden crown decorated with a cherub atop his cowled head. His throne is tall backed and decorated with carved images of butterflies. Though his left hand rests on his knee, his right hand holds an upright sword. He is self-possessed and authoritative, while his double-edged sword suggests an ability to see both sides.

UPRIGHT

Authority, discipline, rationality

•

REVERSED

Coldness, weakness, cruelty

THE
SUIT OF
PENTACLES

The Pentacles are associated with earthly and material concerns, from wealth to work and beyond

When Pentacles feature heavily in a reading, many will think of money and finances, but there's more to them than that. Associated with the element of earth, these worldly cards convey messages relating not only to financial matters, but to security and health too. Pentacles speak to us about the way we interact with and shape our surroundings, whether that's our environment, worldly possessions or career.

Perhaps unsurprisingly, given their connection to money and prosperity, when the Pentacles are seen in less than positive positions, they can signify the negative impact money can have on our lives. Whether a querent is focusing on their career at the expense of other aspects of their life, such as their relationships or even their health, or they are too materialistic or even greedy and Scrooge-like when it comes to money, the Pentacles can carry a warning that we should rethink our priorities. Should the Pentacles be predominant in a reading, it's likely that the querent is concerned with material issues, for better or worse.

> "These cards convey messages relating to financial matters, security and health"

ACE OF
PENTACLES

CARD

A hand emerges from a cloud against a clear sky. Cupped in the palm of the hand is a single gold pentacle. On the ground beneath the hand, the grass is green and verdant, and new white flowers are blooming. A path winds away towards an emerald-green hedgerow, which is studded with red flowers, and the path passes beneath an archway of foliage. On the horizon is a distant mountain.

UPRIGHT

Prosperity, opportunity, new starts

REVERSED

Failed investments, opportunities missed, financial worries

TWO OF
PENTACLES

CARD

A young man holds a pentacle in each hand, the two of them looped around with a green thread. Though he's managing to keep the two pentacles balanced for now, the young man appears to be having to adjust his stance to maintain that stability and not drop either of them. In the distance is a stormy sea, and two boats are tossed on the choppy waters. The clear sky above promises that the storm will soon pass.

UPRIGHT

Juggling priorities, dealing with change, weighing decisions

REVERSED

Lack of organisation, too many balls in the air

THREE OF
PENTACLES

CARD

A stonemason is working in a cathedral, chipping
away at the stone wall. A priest and a robed man are watching,
holding what appear to be the plans that
the man is realising. Above their heads, an elaborate design of three
pentacles is carved into the archway.
Although work is ongoing, it's clear from the impressive stonework that
their working partnership is a fruitful one that will pay dividends.

UPRIGHT

Collaboration, creation, teamwork

REVERSED

Conflict, apathy, rivalry

FOUR OF
PENTACLES

CARD

A man is sitting on a bench, staring out at the querent. He holds a
pentacle protectively, while another pentacle rests atop his crown
and two others are on the ground beneath his feet. Though there is
a whole town behind him, he is alone. The man is entirely focused on
holding on to his pentacles and making sure that nobody can take
them from him, even if that means he cannot move at all.

UPRIGHT

Security, materialism, possessive

REVERSED

Generous, giving, overspending

FIVE OF
PENTACLES

CARD

From behind an ornate stained-glass window showing five pentacles, a bright light shines. Outside, however, the sky is dark and a heavy snow falls onto the already snow-covered ground. A woman wrapped in rags is trudging beneath the window on bare feet. A boy struggles along behind her, resting his weight on crutches. The people are struggling, but they are pressing onwards, looking for sanctuary against the odds.

•

UPRIGHT

Struggle, unemployment, hardship

•

REVERSED

Overcoming adversity, moving on, forgiveness

SIX OF
PENTACLES

CARD

Six pentacles hang in the sky above three people. One of the men is richly dressed and holds a set of scales in one hand, whilst from the other he is distributing coins. Kneeling on the ground before him are two beggars, their hands cupped to receive the coins. Both of the beggars wear blankets, whilst one has a bandaged head. They look at the man with gratitude, and he looks on them with kindness.

•

UPRIGHT

Charity, generosity, giving help

•

REVERSED

Lack of charity, expecting payback, dishonesty

SEVEN OF
PENTACLES

CARD

A young man is taking a break from digging in his garden, resting his hands atop a spade that is buried deep within the earth. He is looking with satisfaction at the bush he has cultivated, upon which six pentacles grow. Another pentacle is on the ground at his feet, suggesting that he has harvested one of the fruits of his labour, while he has decided to let the rest keep growing.

UPRIGHT

Growth, reward, reaping the benefits

•

REVERSED

Lacking effort, abandoning projects, feeling unrewarded

EIGHT OF
PENTACLES

CARD

A young man is sitting on a bench, etching a gold disc with a pentacle. Six completed pentacles are hanging on the tree in front of him, while another is on the ground at his feet. Far in the distance is a town, but he is content to work alone in his own space to ensure he doesn't experience any distractions. He isn't content with the work already done, and is striving to produce more pentacles.

UPRIGHT

Expertise, honed skills, talent

•

REVERSED

Laziness, lacking skill, letting quality slide

NINE OF
PENTACLES

CARD

A woman stands in a vineyard, wearing a rich robe and surrounded by blossoming grapevines where pentacles hang amongst the grapes. A snail is at her feet, and the sky above is rich and golden, with a castle just visible in the background. The woman wears a glove, upon which is perched a hooded falcon. She is enjoying the fruits of her labour and has clearly been richly rewarded for her efforts.

UPRIGHT

Independence, reward, self-reliance

·

REVERSED

Overspending, financial struggles, lacking self-control

TEN OF
PENTACLES

CARD

An old man wearing decorated robes sits before an archway that is decorated with coats of arms and other heraldic symbols. He is petting two dogs while a couple and child are standing in the arch, completing the scene that apparently depicts three generations of the same family. Behind the family we can see an impressive house that, combined with the opulence of their dress and surroundings, suggests that the old man has prepared excellent foundations for his family.

UPRIGHT

Stability, family, affluence

·

REVERSED

Domestic instability, debt

PAGE OF
PENTACLES

CARD

A young man stands alone in a meadow dotted with flowers, beneath a golden sky. Though the distant horizon shows a mountain, closer by are flourishing trees and a ploughed field, ready to produce crops. The young man is focusing all his attention on the pentacle that he holds up in both hands. His dedicated attention suggests that he is ready to start his journey, with a clear focus on what he wants to achieve.

·

UPRIGHT

Loyalty, consistency, ambition

·

REVERSED

Laziness, lack of direction, immaturity

KNIGHT OF
PENTACLES

CARD

A knight in armour sits on a black horse, focused on the pentacle that he holds in his hand. This knight is not charging ahead, unlike the other knights in the tarot pack, but is instead surveying his land and the freshly ploughed fields that will, hopefully, soon be providing him with crops. This knight's adventuring is done for now, and he has decided to concentrate on his work at home.

·

UPRIGHT

Hard work, patience, efficiency

·

REVERSED

Irresponsible, lazy, dull

QUEEN OF
PENTACLES

CARD

A woman sits upon a stone throne that is decorated with carved animals and fruit, beneath a floral archway. The sky is golden and she is surrounded by richly flowering plants, with a rabbit dashing through the image. Above her is a golden sky, while calm streams flow into the horizon. The woman holds a pentacle on her lap, nurturing it and gazing at it with peaceful satisfaction. She is clearly deeply connected to the earth and her surroundings.

·

UPRIGHT

Luxury, comfort, nurture

·

REVERSED

Greed, selfishness, envy

KING OF
PENTACLES

CARD

The man on this card is clearly a great success. Though he wears robes decorated with grapes, the armour beneath suggests that he has a strong sense of self-protection, and the foliage around him, combined with the bulls carved on his throne, tell us that he is a powerful figure. Behind him, an impressive castle provides further proof of his achievements, and he looks on with satisfaction at the pentacle he holds.

·

UPRIGHT

Reliability, security, prosperity

·

REVERSED

Financial irresponsibility, greed, exploitation

THE MISSING MAIDENS

The Cary-Yale Visconti-Sforza deck featured two additional female court cards in each suit

The tarot is full of female figures, from the High Priestess of the Major Arcana to the Queens of each suit. But one particular 15th century deck featured some additions, including the three Virtues – Faith, Hope and Charity – and two unique female archetypes in each suit.

In the 1400s Milan's ruling ducal family commissioned a number of tarot decks; the incomplete remnants of which are referred to as the Visconti-Sforza decks. In the 20th century one of these became part of the collection of Melbert Brinckerhoff Cary Jr, an American graphic designer, publisher and importer, and his wife, Mary Flagler Cary, a Standard Oil heiress. After Cary Jr's death, the widowed Mary presented the couple's historically important playing card collection to Yale University in 1967, and what is now known to tarot aficionados as the Cary-Yale deck became part of the Beinecke Rare Book and Manuscript Library.

This deck adds two extra female figures to each suit. They are the Damsel (sometimes known as the Maid or Maiden, and equivalent to the Page or Knave), and the Horsewoman (sometimes known as the Mounted Damsel or Mounted Lady, and equivalent to the Knight) of Arrows (Wands), Cups, Swords, and Coins (Pentacles).

We don't know why this particular deck includes these additional prominent female figures. The most common theory is that the deck was commissioned as a gift for a highly placed woman in the Milanese court. They're commonly dated to between 1428 and 1447, although one researcher has suggested 1442 to 1447 based on the design of the currency in the Coins suit, while others have theorised that they were actually the first deck commissioned by Filippo Maria Visconti, the Duke of Milan, and are thus the oldest of the Visconti-Sforza decks. Whichever is the case, the date range puts them squarely in the lifetime of Bianca Maria

Bianca Maria Visconti is sometimes known as Lady Tarot as it's thought her father and husband commissioned the unique decks of cards as gifts for her

Visconti, Filippo's only surviving, and illegitimate, daughter. Her husband Francesco I Sforza became Duke of Milan on Filippo's death, and carried on his late father-in-law's project of commissioning tarot decks. Perhaps they were gifts for Bianca Maria – the Horsewomen in particular would certainly have appealed to the Duchess, who was a keen rider and hunter.

The Damsels and Horsewomen were created before tarot became a divination tool, when it was still solely a playing-card game, and as such they have no established occult or arcane meaning. Reproductions of the Cary-Yale card deck are available however, including the Damsels and Horsewomen, and like all tarot cards, if used regularly, your interpretation of each card will soon become apparent.

READING THE CARDS

Learn how to lay out and interpret the cards for a range of queries

READING THE TAROT

Reading the tarot is something anyone can do with just a little bit of practice, and it all starts with learning the basics

When novice tarot readers sit down for the first time with a deck and prepares to make their very first foray into the mysteries and delights of the deck, it is both a daunting and thrilling time. Yet as the reality of learning the meanings, interplay and nuances of each of the 78 cards that make up the tarot pack dawns, it can seem like an almost insurmountable obstacle. Yet that needn't be the case. Just like any skill, learning to read the tarot just takes a little bit of discipline and practice, and every minute spent working with the cards will help to improve the skills and understanding necessary to become a confident tarot reader, regardless of who the reading might be for.

Reading the cards starts with choosing a deck that really speaks to you. For many people, the journey begins with the ever-popular Rider-Waite deck. This is a particularly good choice for someone who is completely new to the tarot simply because it is used by so many websites, books and even tarot tutors as the model deck for newcomers. Plus, its artwork and symbolism influenced innumerable decks that came after, and its universal achetypes can easily be recognised in other decks, regardless of the names of the suits or the deck design. However, whilst the Rider-Waite is without a doubt the most popular, it doesn't have to be the pack that a new reader turns to for their first experiences. There is no hard and fast rule to follow, so long as the reader chooses a deck that appeals to them at a gut level.

Of course, the cards have to be thoroughly shuffled before they can be used for a reading. For some this is imperative to cleanse the energy of the deck, whilst to others it simply offers a kind of reset, wiping away other readings. At a more practical level, it also ensures that the cards are thoroughly random when they're drawn, offering a clean and clear personalised reading. When it comes to shuffling methods, every reader has their own and they range from the fancy card sharping shuffles more common at the card tables of Las Vegas to a more workaday shuffle as one might employ before a game of solitaire. Still other readers welcome the most random approach of all, and simply let their cards fall from their hands to a table or floor, a process

> *Just like any skill, learning to read the tarot just takes a little bit of discipline and practice*

known as scrambling. Once the cards have landed face down, they gather them up again, preserving upright and reversed cards and ensuring a truly random order. Readers may then cut the pack into three piles or invite the querant to do so, perhaps knocking on the back of the upper card with their knuckles whilst stating the intent or question of the reading. Regardless of how it is done, the key ingredient is that a tarot reader does what works for them. For some, that's an esoteric approach in which their cards are stored in silken bags alongside cleansing crystals and only laid out on a silken cloth. For others, keeping the cards in a simple box and laying out a spread on the kitchen table will pay dividends every time.

Whilst choosing and shuffling cards is the start of a tarot journey, learning to interpret them is where the work – and pleasure – really comes in. With nearly eighty cards in

> ## "Whilst choosing and shuffling is the start of a tarot journey, learning to interpret is where the work - and pleasure - comes in"

every tarot pack it can seem like an impossible task, but it doesn't and shouldn't have to be a chore. Each card has a different meaning depending on whether it is upright or reversed (upside down) when it is drawn, and often the meaning can be interpreted at its most basic level simply by examining the imagery on the card. Of course, it isn't a journey that has to be undertaken alone and there are a wealth of resources available to help with understanding. Most decks come with their own quick start guide, and from social media to forums, there are plenty of other readers out there ready to share their understanding and enthusiasm. Whilst written guides can be a great place to start, offering a guiding hand as a novice reader takes their first steps, they're no substitute for experience. As with most hobbies, the best way to improve is to do it and tarot reading is no different.

Tarot is a skill that isn't only learned, but is also intuitive and instinctive. Each reader may see something personal in their cards and interpret them accordingly. Because tarot speaks to and about the deepest part of ourselves and our experience, every reader and querent's personal interpretation is a valuable building block in their understanding of the cards and their relationship to them. One of the wonderful things about tarot is that one cannot ever learn all of the facts by rote; there is no right or wrong answer, and learning about the cards never stops for any reader.

When it comes to laying out the cards to read them, the tarot reader will look for a spread. There are spreads for literally everything, from the classic three card spread or the Celtic Cross to more elaborate layouts that offer guidance on anything from health to career and everything in between. Many tarot practitioners draw a single card once a day and reflect on its significance to their experience, which offers a really practical, simple and easy to adapt way of establishing working with tarot as part of the daily routine.

There are no hard and fast rules when it comes to tarot. Instead, skills flourish when intuition and instinct takes over

However you shuffle and store the cards, the most important thing is that it is the right way for you

> Spreads offer readers an unparalleled opportunity to read the cards as a story

Some readers will only ever use the cards for themselves, whilst others will branch out and begin to read for others

Interpreting the cards might seem like a daunting task, but in reality it is one of the most rewarding skills one can develop

SUPERSTITIONS OF THE TAROT

Perhaps unsurprisingly, the world of tarot is steeped in superstition and some of these arcane beliefs actively discourage novice enthusiasts from really getting to grips with the cards. Unfortunately, one superstition in particular stops some people from picking up a deck before they even have a chance to do so.

One of the most oft-repeated superstitions is that it is bad luck to buy your own tarot deck. Instead, says the old belief, the deck should be given as a gift in order to avoid ill fortune or simply a deck that doesn't work as it should. But nothing could be further from the truth. It's vital that a reader responds to and can connect to the imagery on the cards they work with, so browsing through the decks on offer and choosing one that they fall in love with is a really easy way to ensure that they're happy with their cards. Whilst it's always nice to receive a gift, when it comes to getting hold of a new tarot pack there's no need to wait for someone else to take the hint. Instead, hit the shops, grab that deck that you love and start reading!

Buying your own tarot deck doesn't bring bad luck, but it does offer a tarot reader a chance to choose something that really speaks to them

As with interpreting the cards, tarot spreads don't have to be set in stone. Whilst some of the tried and tested spreads certainly pay dividends, many tarot readers like to develop their own personal spreads as their confidence grows. Spreads offer readers an unparalleled opportunity to read the cards as a story, relating their meanings to one another to build a narrative that will offer guidance whatever the question. No card exists in a vacuum when it appears in a spread, and should be read in relation to those that surround it. Depending on what they are, their influence will subtly shift the outcome of the reading.

Once a reader has gained confidence with interpreting the cards and laying out spreads, some might decide to branch out and start conducting readings for other people. Reading for friends can offer a wonderful opportunity to take one's skills to a new level in a safe and supportive environment. For some people, however, tarot will remain a solo activity and once again, there are no right and wrong approaches. Tarot rewards each reader differently and each person's relationship with the cards is different, just as each person

will have a different ritual for storing, shuffling, cutting and laying out their deck. Reading tarot isn't an exact science, but a skill that each person will learn in a way that best suits them.

When it comes to choosing a tarot deck and sitting down for the first time to get to know the cards, those 78 images might seem impossible to ever tell apart, let alone learn to interpret. Yet interpreting the cards and their relationships to their suits and one another is a process that will soon offer immense rewards. Learning to read the tarot cards, regardless of the deck you choose, is a skill that brings with it new ways of looking at the world and oneself. Perhaps best of all, it isn't something that a person can get wrong. In fact, no matter how they approach it, they can do so safe in the knowledge that the path they choose will be the right path for them. Ultimately, once they've put down their guidebook, picked up their cards and started to get to know them, a world of learning and insight await. This uniquely rewarding hobby is one that anybody can do, with a simple deck of cards and a little time to spend understanding them.

SINGLE CARD SPREAD

A single card can reveal whatever you need it to, from a simple meditation prompt, to daily guidance or clarity over an issue that is causing you stress

PULLING A
SINGLE CARD

A quickfire way to decide your day and clarify your deepest desires

A single card spread is the easiest and quickest way to find answers with the tarot, and familiarise yourself with the cards. This method involves shuffling the cards in your deck and drawing one out, either from the centre of the pack or from the top – much like when you pick from a pack of playing cards from a magician. While you shuffle the cards between your hands, think of a question you need to answer or simply focus on your intention for the card. Or, ask the person you are reading for to do the same and use intuition to select the card that stands out to you. Alternatively, you can spread your deck out in front of you, face down, and use a crystal pendulum to choose your card. Once you have selected your card, lay it down, look at it and reflect. Use your instincts to interpret it before looking up its more esoteric associations. Picking one card allows you to focus on the meanings and interpret it thoroughly. Note down your card in a journal if this helps you progress in learning the tarot. And remember, don't put it back and pick another card if you don't like the one you got – the first card revealed itself to you for a reason!

QUESTION TIPS

When asking the tarot, look deep inside yourself and attempt to compose your thoughts as clearly as possible. The tarot goes beyond the mere surface, and will bring answers to questions that might lay in your unconscious mind. Therefore, it is easier to interpret the tarot if your question is clear, particularly when your answer lies in just one card. Focus on an aspect of life you need to find clarity or guidance. While the tarot will not bring simple yes or no answers, it will point towards a positive or negative outcome. Generic neverending questions such as "will I ever find Mr Right?" or "will I become a success?" will not bring about answers. Try asking "will pursuing X result in X?" or "will I succeed in X by this time next year?"

PROMPTING YOUR PRACTISE

Perhaps you want to use it as a daily prompt or guidance, a meditation cue or even pick a 'destiny' card to guide you for the following year or years ahead. A single card spread is great if you want to pick a daily card that can function as a meditation or spell prompt, or to give guidance towards your day. If picking a daily card, simply set your intention that you want a card for the day or ask a question, like "what do I need to know today?" Perhaps ask the cards to show you what the most important thing you need to work on is, either today or in life at this moment.

When using it for a meditation prompt, set this intention when shuffling and focus on every aspect of the card, its colours, any hidden imagery, the shapes, the numbers. Focusing on something visual while practising yogic breathing techniques or using a body scan method can help switch the rest of your mind off and reclaim control over the woes of daily life, even if you only have time for one to ten minutes a day. For spellcasting, repeat the spell or the goal of said spell as you select your card. You can also draw a single card in order to inspire your writing or art when you are stuck for inspiration.

EITHER/OR

A variation of this method (technically a two-card spread) that works for quick decision making, is to split your deck into two equal piles, or alternatively, if you have them, use two decks (preferably of the same type). Nominate each pile for one possibility or outcome and shuffle both piles. Read the card off the top of each pile to decide which possibility or outcome is preferable – if any!

— PULLING A —
THREE CARD SPREAD

A good way to get perspective and insight on
past, present and future

A three-card spread is a popular layout for beginners, or those seeking more in-depth advice in a hurry. This spread offers insight into the progression of a given situation, and is more often than not used in a past/present/future layout format. However, you can pretty much nominate each card in the layout with whatever label you so choose. For example, a situation/action/outcome spread.

There are two ways to create a three-card spread. The first way is to separate your pack into three equal piles and turn the top card of each pile upwards. The second way is to shuffle your cards and select three cards from the main pile, lay them out next to each other and turn each one to face upwards, one after the other. It doesn't matter which technique you use, just do what feels right for you. Of course, as with all tarot spreads, it is important to focus on your question or situation as you shuffle the cards!!

INTERPRETING YOUR CARDS

The most common reading of a three-card spread is past/present/future or basis of the matter-near future-outcome. In this reading, the first card represents what has already come to pass, or the events and circumstances that have led up to where you are now. The second card represents the present situation you are in and how you feel about it, or perhaps a new direction or condition that will soon come into fruition. The third card is the outcome or future, representing the end result or resolve of the situation. This spread is very useful for financial matters, issues concerning your career path or other difficult decisions and situations that may be occurring in your life.

For example, you lay out a spread of past/present/future for a question regarding financial matters and turn the cards Ace of Pentacles/the Devil/the Sun. Card one is an Ace, representing fresh starts. The basis of the matter is new investments or money that you have invested that was held up but recently received. Card two is the Devil, a Major Arcana card that always signifies an important event. You are stuck in a negative cycle of events and are struggling to see clearly and perceive the whole picture. You may have been seduced by the material world and made a mistake with your finances; unexpected losses and major financial difficulties have plagued you, but you will soon receive another opportunity to make more money, just use discretion from here on out. Card three is the future outcome, in this case, it is the Sun. The Sun's focus is on people and society, achievement and accomplishment, indicating that your financial situation will be sorted. New money will come in and the anguish that has plagued you will finally be rewarded.

ROMANCE AND SELF LOVE

For matters of the heart, you may wish to use a different three-card spread, for example you/them/relationship outcome spread or relationship positives/relationship negatives/where the relationship is headed. The three-card spread can also be used for self discovery and personal growth. You may want to delve into the cards to help bring up unconscious thoughts and feelings, and learn where you may need to head or aspects of yourself that need working on. For example, where you stand in terms of your mind/body/spirit, where you are/where you are headed now/where your potential lies.

CARD 1

The first card could represent the past, a specific situation, your own needs, where you are or the mind, depending on your question

CARD 3

The third card could represent the future, the outcome of a given situation or relationship, where your potential lies or the spirit, depending on your question

CARD 2

The second card could represent the present (or near future), an action you need to take, the feelings of another, where you are headed or the body (physical self), depending on your question

CARD 1

The first card gives insight into the current state of affairs, including aspects of it that you may not be aware of.

CARD 2

The factors which are influencing the area you wish to examine are revealed by this card, including your motivations and desires.

CARD 3

The third card displays the challenges that you are facing in this part of your life and ones which may occur in the future.

CARD 4

This card predicts how things will turn out for you in this area in the long run

CARD 5

The fifth card sits at the heart of the spread and reveals the theme of the entire reading, with its meaning influenced by the surrounding cards.

THE
FIVE CARD
RECTANGLE

When you have a question related to an area of your life, from love to your career, the five-card rectangle can help untangle the situation

Five-card tarot spreads allow for greater insight than simpler spreads. By increasing the number of cards more can be gleaned for the questioner. The five-card rectangle has many uses. It can be used to answer specific questions about an aspect of your life or analyse the general situation in which you find yourself.

The last card to be pulled in the five-card rectangle is sometimes known as the theme card. This fifth card sits at the heart of the spread and its meaning will also be at the heart of the questions you wish to have answered. When used to help understand a relationship this card represents the querent themselves. Indeed the fifth card in the rectangle will usually be closely related to the querent as invariably we have the strongest influence on our own lives.

The first card relates to the present situation of the questioner. Are they in a positive or negative place in this moment? Just as the present is influenced by the past so this card will also point to past factors that may still be at work.

The second card looks more generally at things which may be beyond your control and how they are causing your situation to be in flux. These may be the intentions of other people or their actions, or simply the state of the world and your place in it.

When looking at what challenges are in wait for the querent it is the third card which has the most to say. If you have asked a specific question then this is the card that might point to the biggest obstacles that lay before you. Remember, these difficulties can be ones which we cause ourselves.

When attempting to understand what the final outcome will be for the area under scrutiny the fourth card points the way. This card must be understood in relation to the others which have been pulled. If the answer appears to be negative this could be a warning that you must pursue a different tactic to achieve your goals. Acting in the same way as always will rarely lead to change. A positive card in this place can be guiding a person to remain on the course they are already charting – and a reminder not to lose focus.

> **"The five-card rectangle has many uses - to answer specific questions or analyse the general situation you find yourself in"**

THE
FIVE CARD
CROSS

This configuration of cards helps to unveil the past, present, and future of a situation – particularly where relationships are involved

When consulting tarot cards about a romantic relationship perhaps the most common spread used is the five-card cross. The layout is straightforward and easy to remember and it has a relatively simple set of steps in its interpretation. Many tarot users will use this spread at the beginning of a new romance to glimpse potential outcomes. It can also be used to answer specific problems that arise later between two people. Some will also use the five-card cross to examine platonic relationships they have with others in their lives, such as a family member or colleague.

As the querent thinks about a relationship, and any particular problems they may be having, the five cards are drawn from the deck and placed in a cross form. The middle three cards work very much in the same way as a simple three-card spread and represent the past, present, and future. Here, they help to reveal facets of a relationship that the querent may not have consciously considered, as well as its eventual outcome.

The fourth and fifth cards give this spread its deeper insight. The fourth card does not just represent the current state of a relationship but delves into the foundations of the romance. If the querent has a specific question about the relationship they want answered it is this card that reveals the reasons they are asking the question in the first place.

The fifth card relates to the potential in a relationship. It points towards what is ultimately possible for those involved and how a person might work to achieve the best outcome. It may also reveal the unconscious and underlying issues in the relationship that need to be addressed.

The third card, which represents the future, may not always give the querent the result of their relationship that will come true. It may be pointing towards a possibility for the relationship if things do not change. A positive third card can be drawn when all the other cards hint at negativity. This is a sign that by taking actions to current problems the relationship may have a happy ending.

If the tarot points to a positive past but an uncertain future, or even a disastrous outcome, it may be a hint that the querent needs to change back to a way of thinking, feeling, or acting that they had in the past.

> **"The middle three cards work in the same way as a simple three-card spread, representing the past, present and future"**

CARD 4

The fourth card relates to the reasons that current circumstances in the relationship exist and why the querent is focused on them.

CARD 1

This card represents the past and the things which you bring to the relationship and your role in it.

CARD 2

The present state of the relationship is revealed by this card, and the issues which may exist between you.

CARD 5

This card points to the foundations of your relationship as well as the potential for you to overcome the known and unknown barriers between lovers.

CARD 3

The present state of the relationship is revealed by this card, and the issues which may exist between you.

CARD 3

Hidden influences reign in this card. These can range from the actions of other people to the querent's own subconscious.

CARD 5

The attitudes of others can be vital to understanding what we should do and this card reveals the intentions of those around you.

CARD 4

The fourth card points to obstacles that may occur to the querent relating to the question which has been asked.

CARD 2

The second card represents the present condition that the querent is in and how the querent is feeling about it.

CARD 6

What should the querent do? This is the card which will tell you what should be done to achieve your goal.

CARD 1

The past finds its expression in this card – both events and influences that have brought about the current situation are revealed.

CARD 7

The seventh card predicts the future and the ultimate outcome of the querent's actions – so long as the cards are heeded.

THE
SEVEN CARD
HORSESHOE

When unsure about a question or situation the seven-card horseshoe can tease out meanings and answers from many possibilities

The seven-card horseshoe is one of the most popular tarot spreads for querents who need answers when they are unsure what to do. By examining the cards that are pulled a querent is offered a full view of a given situation, its past influences, and the final result of their actions.

Reading the cards in order is relatively simple as they follow a direct line from the past, to the present, to difficulties ahead, to what the questioner should actually do. As with most tarot spreads, however, one must be careful not to do too literal a reading as the interplay between the cards must be fully recognised to be understood.

The first card tells the querent about key parts of their past which are still acting on their present predicament. These can be things which occurred long ago and have left emotional and intellectual marks on a person or more recent events that will play directly into the situation. The second card, which represents the present, can help understand the first by looking at the relationship between them. This card also delves into the feelings the querent has towards the topic they are concerned with.

The third and fourth cards help the questioner recognise unexplored factors in making their decision. The third card addresses the hidden influences which may be interfering in their life. These unseen elements in the question can spring from both the actions of others and a person's own subconscious feelings. The fourth card represents the obstacles that are standing in the way of the querent. Again, these could be external problems or ones that a querent is struggling to deal with inside themselves.

The fifth card directly interrogates the intentions of others towards the querent. The attitude of others shapes the environment we all live in. By seeing how others are disposed towards you and in regard to the question asked you are better able reach your goals.

When people turn to the seven-card horseshoe spread it's usually because they are uncertain what the best course of action is – revealed by the sixth card. It may suggest a bold move, something more subtle, or simply perseverance. Its guidance must be understood in conjunction with the other cards.

The seventh card tells the querent what the outcome of their actions, if they follow the prompting of the cards, will be. A positive card here can be a sign to pay greater heed to the other cards, while a negative one may suggest that the question or your attitude to it needs to be re-evaluated.

> **"The seven-card horseshoe offers a full view of a given situation, its past influences and the final result of a querent's actions"**

THE
TWELVE CARD
ASTROLOGICAL SPREAD

When performed at the beginning of the year this spread can reveal the factors which will influence the coming cycle of the zodiac

There are many influences which act on our life and many are not always easy to recognise or understand. By using the twelve-card astrological spread a querent seeks to frame the answers offered by tarot within the guiding frame of the zodiac. These can be as simple as using this to get insight into what the year will bring on a month-by-month basis. Others prefer to interpret the cards they draw in relation to the astrological signs they represent.

The circular nature of this spread not only echoes the circle of the zodiac which moves in the heavens but also symbolises the patterns of our lives. By focusing on the passage of the year a person is able to examine their goals and aspirations. With a close reading of the cards the course of the upcoming year and how each factor will feed into it is disclosed. This makes the twelve-card astrological spread one of the more complex tarot spreads to interpret.

As well as the intrinsic meanings of the cards in the tarot in this spread a user must also construe what they are saying in light of the zodiac sign they are representing. For instance a negative card drawn in Libra can suggest an imbalance in some aspect of your life that will occur. It could also be a warning that a person must be on guard against allowing imbalances to form in the first place.

The twelve-card astrological spread is thought to also be one of the most personal of tarot spreads. The force of the zodiac on a person's identity means that this spread represents deeply individual needs, desires, and psychological states. Of course this makes it all the more powerful as it gives observations that suggest how an individual's talents and potential can be used.

With so many levels of interpretation available this is a tarot spread that rewards repeated pondering. When all the possible meanings have been teased from the cards a person is left with a more complete understanding of themselves and their place in the world.

Some who use this spread also draw a thirteenth card which they place in the centre of the circle. This is the theme card. This may give a glimpse at the general outlook for the year ahead or can be used to interpret the other cards in the spread by seeing how the theme card may influence and modify their meaning.

> **"The force of the zodiac on a person's identity means that this spread represents deeply individual needs and desires"**

PISCES
What things are you ignoring or unable to deal with? This card will point them out and suggest how to exorcise them.

ARIES
This card represents both how you define yourself and how you are projecting yourself to others.

GEMINI
This card deals with thought and communication and reveals how they should be incorporated into decisions.

CAPRICORN
Those in need of practical advice should look here as it can also warn of distractions that will lead them astray.

TAURUS
If you want to know what guides you and what you value this card will reveal it.

AQUARIUS
This card deals with a person's relationship with humanity in general and offers new opportunities for a fresh start.

LEO
This card represents possible conflicts but also deals with passions and expressions of personality.

SCORPIO
The Scorpio card can represent endings but also hints at changes that need to be made to move forward.

SAGITTARIUS
Deeper meanings and transitions are found in this card – long-term goals and aims are found here.

CANCER
The Cancer card reveals issues of safety, security, and how a person should meet their goals without danger.

LIBRA
Libra represents balance and in this spread this card reveals the state of relationships and how best to be fair.

VIRGO
When consulting about health and well-being this card shows the way in which all aspects of life can be nurtured.

FUTURE

This card presents the many possibilities which are open to the querent to give guidance about what options they may choose.

PRESENT

This card reveals the current state of affairs in the querent's life as well as their state of mind.

PAST

This card represents the paths and actions which have led to the situations a person is facing at this moment.

THE PILLAR

OUTCOME

The final result of the current situation is revealed here – though it may be changed if the querent changes their actions.

HOPES AND FEARS

This card deals with the twin factors of hope and fear within the querent to show how they may influence the outcome.

CHALLENGE

This card uncovers the most pressing problems facing the querent which, if resolved, would improve their life.

SUBCONSCIOUS

The ideas, desires, and hopes bubbling away underneath a person's mind with be revealed by this card.

THE CROSS

NEAR FUTURE

Those things which will happen soon, and are already taking shape, are found in this card.

EXTERNAL FACTORS

The people and energies which will shape the outcome of the question at hand are shown in this card.

INTERNAL FACTORS

This card represents the person asking the question and their state of mind. What is your view of your ability to change your life?

THE
CELTIC CROSS

This complex spread might seem intimidating at first, but once mastered it offers profound insight into the subconscious

This tarot spread gets its name from the central cross and pillar of Celtic crosses that are found in Ireland from at least the 9th century. By drawing on this ancient symbol, early users of tarot were able to design a spread that allows for one of the deepest readings. When a querent wants to interrogate a question from many angles and understand it fully it is often the Celtic cross that they turn to.

The first recorded mention of the Celtic cross spread comes from 1911 in Arthur Edward Waite's important work The Pictorial Key to the Tarot. He describes it as "an ancient Celtic method of divination" and suggests that it is best used by those with clearly defined questions. Waite also says that it is one of the more potent ways of reading tarot because it deals with questions that are "free from all complications."

The cards of the Celtic cross spread can be read one-by-one as they are drawn. For those who wish to extract the most information they can however the relationships between the cards and what they represent must be taken into account.

The spread is split into two main parts. The cross is formed from the first six cards that are drawn. These represent the present situation and all the factors that have lead to the current state of affairs. At the heart of the cross is a smaller cross formed by cards one and two. These cards are central to the question being asked – they refer to the questioner and the challenges they will face.

Cards three and five are sometimes called the Above and Below cards, echoing the famous alchemical saying "as above, so below." These two cards represent the conscious and subconscious mind. Here, the relationship between the two cards will tell a questioner if they are at war with themselves. They may offer ideas on how to bring your conscious goals into agreement with your true, unconscious desires.

The pillar is created by the four final cards laid out in a vertical line. These offer further insights into all the things which lay behind the question the querent is asking. This gives the querent the background that they need to judge the meaning of the other cards.

The Subconscious (card three) may be hard to understand. By looking to card number nine (Hopes and Fears) in the pillar a querent can get a better understanding of what it is telling them. Our hopes and fears often spring from our subconscious. By looking at both cards in tandem it can help to interpret each card and see how best to move forward.

The Future card (card five) can best be viewed in relation to card ten – the Outcome. Are they both positive? Then this means that the querent is acting in a way that will lead to the best possible result. When the Future card is negative but the Outcome card is positive it can be pointing out that the querent can make active changes that will allow the to reach the best outcome. When this mismatch between the two cards exists then all cards should be looked at carefully to fully examine what aspects of the querent might be contributing to the unhappy outcome.

Card eight is the External Factors card. These are often things outside of the querent's control. If they are negative then it can mean that they are simply something that must be accepted before a situation can be resolved.

As with all tarot spreads there are no easy answers that come from the Celtic cross. Mastering its use and unveiling its meanings takes time and deep contemplation.

"The Celtic cross is one of the more potent ways of reading tarot"

When a tarot card comes out reversed this can change its meaning, but this isn't necessarily a bad thing

The Hanged Man can be a tricky one for novice readers – he hangs upside-down, which can make you think the card is reversed!

REVERSED CARDS

When tarot cards come out upside-down, the changes to their established meanings can add nuance and context to a reading

When you (or the person you're reading for) has shuffled the tarot cards thoroughly, not all of them will be the right way up any more. When these come out in a reading, these cards are known as reversed. Some tarot readers prefer not to read reversals, and simply turn any upside-down cards the right way round; many novice readers are advised to stick to upright card meanings until they've mastered the basics of laying out and interpreting the cards. But for many, reversed cards can bring an extra layer of nuance and meaning to a reading.

The reason some readers don't like to engage with reversals is because they are sometimes thought of as having a negative or shadowy aspect, the opposite of the card's upright meaning. But not all tarot cards are positive when they're the right way up. The Nine of Swords, for example, can denote grief, vulnerability, and suffering. Reversed, however, it can point to a way out of these issues, a light at the end of the tunnel where the Nine of Swords is no longer hanging over one's head. Not all reversed cards have negative meanings.

> Most cards have a symmetrical design on the back so you can't tell if you've pulled a reversed card until you've turned it over

Reversed cards stand out in a spread, and so some readers think of this as drawing even more attention to their meaning. In this case the reader needs to ask, how does the reversed card meaning relate to the querent's question, and what is its place in the spread? Reversed cards in this context can show blockages and imbalances. If the High Priestess shows up reversed in a spread, for example, it can mean that the card's normal meaning of intuition isn't playing out in the querent's life. It could mean that they need to trust their intuition, or conversely that their instincts are off. The Three of Cups can denote fun and celebrations; reversed it could advise that party time is over, or simply show that the querent needs a little downtime to recharge. Like all readings, the position in the spread and relationship to the surrounding cards will add context to the reversed card's meaning.

Another way to read reversed cards is that their meaning becomes internalised rather than external. The Empress denotes motherliness and care. Reversed, it doesn't have to mean the opposite of this and become dour and stifling – it could allude to the querent needing to turn that nurturing impulse on themselves rather than outwards to others all the time, and take a moment for some self-care.

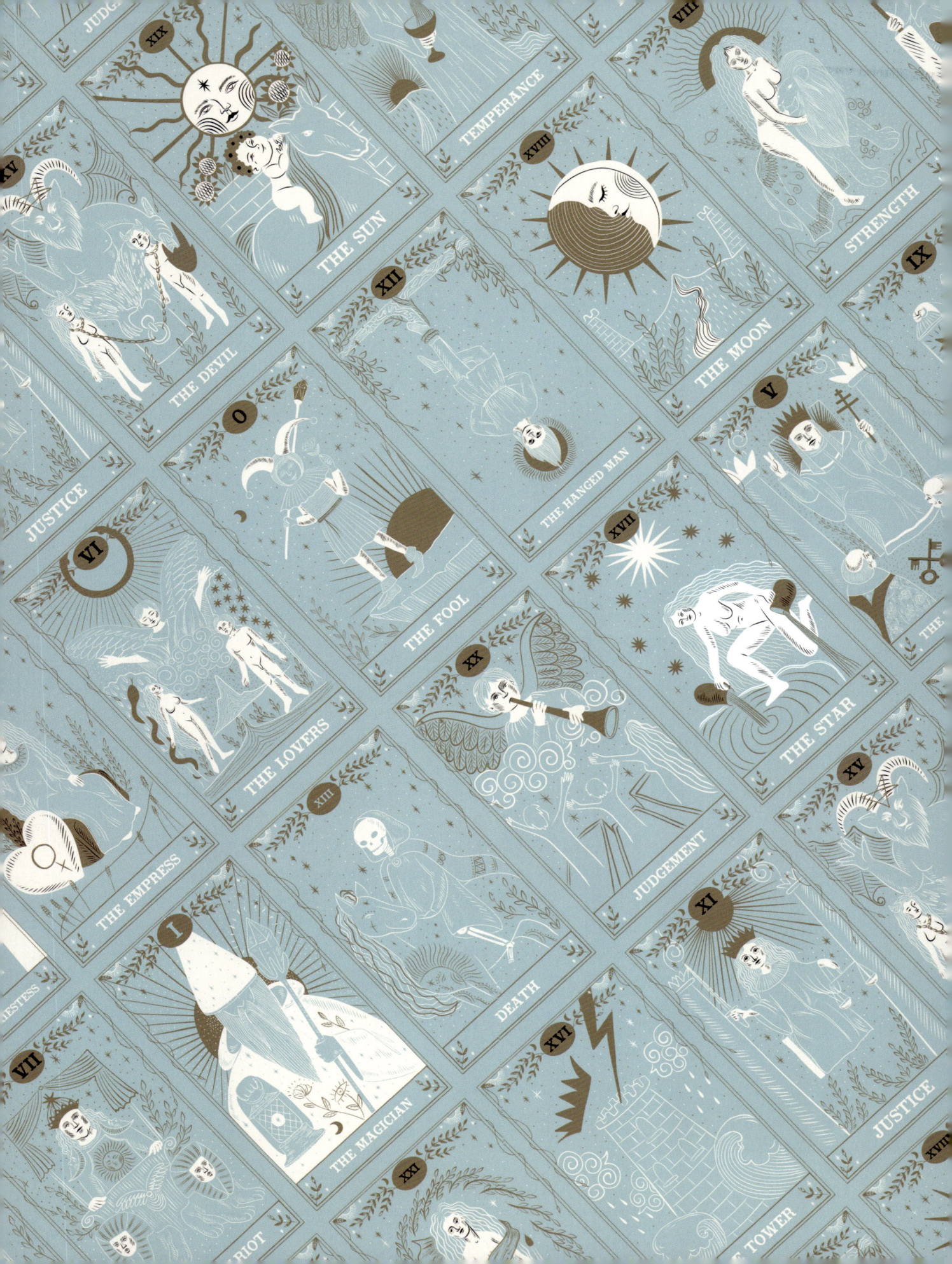